HOW TO BE A . .

SUPERSALESMAN

★

HOW TO BE A...
SUPERSALESMAN

ART LINKLETTER

★★★★

PRENTICE-HALL, INC.
Englewood Cliffs, N.J.

Original art by John DeMarco

How to be a ... Supersalesman
by Art Linkletter
Copyright © 1974 by Art Linkletter
All rights reserved. No part of this book may be
reproduced in any form or by any means, except
for the inclusion of brief quotations in a review,
without permission in writing from the publisher.
Printed in the United States of America
Prentice-Hall International, Inc., London
Prentice-Hall of Australia, Pty. Ltd., North Sydney
Prentice-Hall of Canada, Ltd., Toronto
Prentice-Hall of India Private Ltd., New Delhi
Prentice-Hall of Japan, Inc., Tokyo

10 9 8 7 6 5 4 3 2 1

Library of Congress Cataloging in Publication Data

Linkletter, Arthur Gordon,
  How to be a ... supersalesman.

    1. Salesmen and salesmanship.   2. Persuasion
(Psychology) I. Title.
HF5438.L614   658.8   73–18025
ISBN 0–13–396606–2

**Dedicated to
articulate salesmen
and persuasive communicators
everywhere.**

I wish to acknowledge, with deep appreciation, the superb, creative editing skills of my friend Keith Monroe.

Contents

HOW TO BE A . . .
SUPERSALESMAN

★

1-- *HE COULDN'T GET IN THE DOOR*

Persuasion by Remote Control

Let's imagine that you're a salesman whose job depends on getting the signature of a certain Mr. Big on the dotted line. Mr. Big knows you and knows what you want, but is completely scornful. He won't see you. He won't even accept your phone calls. If you don't sign him up within the next few days, you'll be jobless and broke. What should you do?

This was the problem that Billy Rose faced, and solved, at the turning point of his career. He used a magic sales strategy that became a key to success throughout his life. I've copied it sometimes, and I'm sure you can, too.

When Billy came up against this problem he seemed to have reached the end of his rope. He had lost his life savings producing two costly flops on Broadway. He had wasted six months in a futile search for work in Hollywood. Then he put every dollar he could borrow in a third show. But he suddenly learned that he couldn't get permission to use the one theater in which it could be shown.

The show was *Jumbo*—a gigantic combination musical comedy and circus with a hundred animals, Jimmy Durante, Paul Whiteman, and music by Rodgers and Hart. It was so huge

1

that Billy had to rent a riding academy and the Manhattan Opera House for rehearsals. The only theater big enough to contain it was New York's 4,000-seat Hippodrome, with its 300 stagehands.

Billy had rented the Hippodrome, he thought. But at the last moment the theater owners (the English branch of the aristocratic Astor family) sent word that they had reconsidered.

In their view, Mr. Rose lacked prestige and *Jumbo* lacked dignity. So they decided to rent their Hippodrome instead to Max Reinhardt, a producer famed in Berlin and Vienna. The Astors felt Reinhardt and his drama would be more suitable to their own social standing.

Here was a problem for a supersalesman. The Astors were somewhere abroad, completely unreachable. Their theater was entrusted to a Wall Street banker who was all too familiar with Rose's record of failure, with his obscure niche as a nobody in show business. This was the man whom Billy somehow had to get in to see, and to sell.

The strategy Billy used to accomplish this was basically simple: *Ask your friends to use their influence.*

When you need to approach a seemingly unapproachable prospect, just inquire around. Before long you'll find someone who knows someone who knows Mr. Unapproachable. At the very least you'll thereby be able to get yourself invited to a few club meetings, cocktail parties, or other gatherings where you'll find chances to rub shoulders with Mr. U. and exchange a few words while he's in a relaxed mood. And never forget that almost anyone you know will be glad to put in a kind word for you if asked to do so.

Billy used this simple, often-overlooked fact about human nature to get through closed doors time and again. He had to use it to the utmost to get into the Hippodrome. "I knew I had to bring in the biggest gun I could think of," he told me long afterward.

So he turned to Bernard M. Baruch, centimillionaire, Wall

Street operator, and adviser to presidents. Billy had been Baruch's stenographer when the great man was chairman of the War Industries Board in 1918. Billy was only seventeen then, a high-school dropout, but he already sensed one principle that shrewd old George Bernard Shaw had put into words long ago: "Getting patronage is the whole art of life. A man cannot have a career without it."

HOW TO GET A PATRON

Billy had made Baruch his patron. How? By openly showing admiration for him. He copied the great man's mannerisms and way of speaking; he even wore double-breasted navy blue suits because Baruch did. Billy once explained to me, "I think Bernie thought, 'This little guy's stuck on me and thinks I'm a hell of a fellow.' "

For years whenever Billy needed to impress someone he grabbed a phone, got the long-distance operator, and said, "Connect me with Mr. Baruch. Tell him Billy Rose. . . . Hello, Bernie?" The great financier was ten times more important than anyone in show business and Rose called him Bernie! Who wouldn't be impressed? As for the subject of the call, usually it was just that Billy had tickets down front to this or that show and would Bernie come? Naturally this pleased Baruch and he often did come.

When Billy needed his help in renting the Hippodrome, Baruch was crossing the Atlantic on the *Normandie*. Billy sent him a desperate radiogram (maybe the only time an SOS went from shore to ship). Baruch, glad to show his influence and play the role of benefactor, responded. He sent a message to the president of a giant bank that controlled the Astor bank. Next day the banker who had refused to accept Billy's phone calls invited him in and gave him the keys to the Hippodrome.

His troubles didn't end once he was inside the theater. Pro-

duction problems forced the postponement of the opening five
times. On the day *Jumbo* was at last ready to open, a fireman
inspected the theater and denounced it as a "house of viola-
tions." The show couldn't go on, he ruled.

So again Billy had a sales problem, this time with an officious,
stubborn fireman. Billy used the same technique once more.
Baruch was still out of the country. Billy told an assistant,
"Call Swope."

Herbert Bayard Swope was a legend in New York. As executive editor of Pulitzer's *World,* he had made it one of America's
great newspapers. He was a confidant of Al Smith and Franklin
D. Roosevelt. He golfed with Lord Northcliffe in England and
dined with Queen Marie in Romania. Stanley Walker, another
famous editor, wrote of Swope: "His gift of gab is a torrential
and terrifying thing. He is as easy to ignore as a cyclone."

Twenty minutes after receiving Rose's call, Swope swooped
down on the Hippodrome. As Billy described it, "He blew in
like a north wind. Herbert took that fireman aside and began
talking to him, and I don't know what he said, but pretty soon
he had the fireman charmed and bedazzled, and we opened
that night and played for five months and never had another
such complaint."

Why should a famous, busy man like Swope leave his own
office on a moment's notice and rush to help Billy Rose? For
the same reason that Baruch had helped.

Swope had been vice-chairman of the War Industries Board
when Billy worked there. Billy had enlisted him too as a patron,
by doing extra chores for him after hours and by cultivating
him throughout the 1920s in the same way he did Baruch.
Eventually Swope opened many doors for the youngster. For
example, at Swope's home little Billy Rose (born Rosenberg)
of New York Public School 44 met John Hay Whitney of Yale,
who soon put up hundreds of thousands of dollars to finance
Billy's shows.

Billy Rose

Some people thought Billy went overboard in his zeal to acquire patrons. But I think he was sincere. He genuinely admired successful people and was perfectly natural in showing it.

Thomas Sugrue wrote of him, "His entire success is founded on an immense enthusiasm. He bows and scrapes before the slightest smattering of genius. His employees know exactly what famous person he's been with the night before, because he arrives at his office talking like that person."

Whenever Billy was at a party with witty people he ostentatiously copied down their witticisms in shorthand. For a while he wore a beard in emulation of Jed Harris, the most successful Broadway producer of the era. He affected a twitching cheek because this was a mannerism of a top playwright, Ben Hecht (who did it involuntarily because of a muscle quirk). For anyone but Billy to go to such lengths would have seemed ridiculous, but they were a natural part of his gaudy, headlong way of doing things. In the more relaxed way that's natural for me, I've always let my interest in people show through and I'm glad. It has led me to warm friendships all over the country, just as it did for Billy.

I used to think Billy was a pioneer in the art of acquiring famous benefactors, but I've discovered that a young man named Hall Caine set exactly this pattern in the 1890s. Caine was a blacksmith's son. As did Billy, he had only eight years of school. But he yearned to be a writer. So he picked out a great writer of that day, Dante Gabriel Rossetti, and took aim. He read everything Rossetti wrote and began to give talks in praise of Rossetti's works. He sent a copy of one talk to Rossetti himself, who was so delighted that he invited this blacksmith's son to come to London and be his secretary. It was the turning point in Hall Caine's life. In his new job he met the literary lions of the time, sought their advice and help, and learned how to turn out novels that were huge commercial successes. He became the richest literary man of the century.

ASK HIM ABOUT HIMSELF

Maybe you're thinking, "That might have been okay for Billy Rose or Hall Caine, but I could never approach big shots that way." Think again. Next time you listen to a speech by any well-known person, take a few notes on points that interest you. Then write the speaker a one-page letter asking him an intelligent question about whatever point hit you hardest. I'll bet he answers with a personal letter. And if you want to continue the correspondence in terms of his own interests and opinions, it's more likely than not to lead eventually to a very pleasant relationship. Famous people are human beings. Every human being would rather talk about himself than any other subject, if his listener is genuinely interested.

Let me cite one more famous example to drive the point home. An obscure thirteen-year-old immigrant boy, working as a Western Union messenger, won the personal attention of the biggest men of his day by merely writing a special kind of letter to each of them. He made friends with three U.S. Presidents and the widow of another, two of the Army's top generals, and a dozen other celebrities.

The boy was named Edward Bok. At twenty-six he was to become editor of the *Ladies' Home Journal* and make it a huge success. And it would be one of his pen pals, Rutherford B. Hayes, who as President would break precedent by writing a magazine article for Bok that started him toward success.

What had Bok done to get on friendly terms with dignitaries who were besieged daily by favor-seekers? He had read short biographies of them, then sent them questions about points that interested him in their personal histories.

"With the simple directness of a Dutch boy," a biographer wrote, "Bok asked General James A. Garfield if the story of his once being a boy on the towpath was true, and telling him why he asked. Garfield answered him fully and cordially. Then the idea came to the boy to procure other letters from noted men, for the sake of learning something useful. . . .

"So he started, asking why one man did this or that, or the date of an occurrence in his life. . . . Several authors asked Edward to come and see them."

Many of us must win and hold the attention of big shots who don't know us; we must get through those closed doors. Do we, like Bok and Caine and Billy Rose, think in terms of the big shot's interests?

HOW GO-BETWEENS HELP

Three centuries ago Sir Francis Bacon wrote an essay, "Of Negotiating," in which he advised: "It is generally better to deal by the mediation of a third than by a man's self. Use bold men for expostulation, fair-spoken men for persuasion, crafty men for inquiry and observation, forward and absurd men for business that doth not well bear out itself."

When you think about it, the advantages of having a go-between act for you are obvious. He can talk for you in a way you can't talk yourself. He can negotiate without committing you so that you needn't put all your cards on the table too soon. And he can give you good advice because he sees your problem from a different viewpoint.

Every entertainer uses an agent. Lawyers, realtors, and bargaining representatives make various deals on other people's behalf. Yet we all overlook many other opportunities to get help from a third party. Why shouldn't every salesman ask his customers, suppliers, and personal friends to put in a word for him now and then? Usually they're glad to because it makes them feel more important. (John Dewey, the eminent educator, believed that the desire to be important is the deepest urge in human nature.)

Even in straight business deals a smart negotiator sometimes uses an intermediary when there's no apparent need for one. There is a story about John Niello, who was at one time treasurer of a big manufacturing company. His company needed to borrow $10 million for expansion but didn't want to issue stock or bonds, so Niello decided to get the money in a lump sum from an insurance company. The president of Niello's firm was a friend of the president of an insurance company that was looking for chances to make such loans. You might think that the manufacturing president would just go to the insurance president and arrange the loan. But no. Niello says: "We hired a firm of investment bankers to negotiate it. This cost us more than $50,000 for the investigation and handling of the loan—but we figured it was worthwhile because the investment bankers could talk about us in a way we couldn't, and because we didn't have to commit ourselves until we were sure all arrangements satisfied us. Furthermore, the bank was involved in the loan with us, so it would feel obliged to help if anything went wrong. Suppose we fell behind in payments. The bank would help work out new arrangements, or help find the money elsewhere."

THE KNACK OF NAME-DROPPING

Sometimes merely dropping a few friends' names can help make a sale. Billy discovered this as a youngster, soon after leaving the War Industries Board, when he began writing songs and trying to peddle them to sheet music publishers.

In those days the publishers were lordly men. A composer would wait hours or days in their anterooms for a hearing. After hearing the song, the publisher simply took the scribbled copy and brusquely sent the composer home to pray for a favorable decision, which might or might not come weeks later.

Billy changed this system single-handedly. He had printed

copies of his songs made and phoned publishers for audition dates. He refused to accept just any old date, but parleyed until the publisher set a time on a Saturday or Sunday when there would be no interruption. Billy was able to insist on this because he had made a point of fraternizing with top songwriters and could throw their names around impressively. In fact, he had persuaded one or two well-known tunesmiths to write music for his lyrics, on the understanding that he would be the salesman of the songs.

Before the audition Billy got prominent band leaders to try the song on the public, which helped whet the publishers' interest. And instead of slinking into the audition room, Billy came on as if the publishers had begged him to be there. He brought along a good pianist and some popular tenor to sing the words. But then, after this impressive production, he never tried to make a sale on the spot. Instead he said a brisk goodby, merely advising the publisher to "give it some thought."

Then he went to another company and put on a similar performance, dropping hints about the interest shown by the first publisher. To a third he conveyed the impression that the first and second publishers were fighting for the rights to his song. If one company made an offer, Billy quickly mentioned it to the others. Music-publishing houses were jealous of each other and instinctively tried to prevent a rival from getting a potential hit. So Billy was able to get them bidding against each other and to extract better terms than songwriters ever received before.

ANOTHER LESSON FROM BILLY ROSE

I first met Billy Rose in 1936 when I was an ambitious twenty-three-year-old and he was riding the rainbow. I was directing radio operations for the Texas Centennial Exposition in Dallas for a modest stipend. He was being paid a thousand dollars a day to help Fort Worth stage its own rival Frontier Centennial. He decided to get some technical advice in setting up a public-address system and sent for me.

At our first meeting I began learning a fundamental lesson in showmanship (and salesmanship) although it didn't sink in for a while.

The cocky little showman disagreed with practically every suggestion I made about the public-address system. I soon concluded that he didn't really want any advice from me. It shook my confidence until I realized, on thinking it over, that we were both right. My experience with sound systems had been in places where pleasant background music and unobtrusive announcements were best. But Billy was staging outdoor shows that had to be big, brassy, and "circusy" to succeed. "I don't let 'em think!" Billy insisted. "I give 'em excitement."

His flashy extravaganzas in Fort Worth far outdrew the tasteful historical pageants in Dallas. He put up huge signs, Be Educated in Dallas—Have Fun in Fort Worth. If you were given that choice, which road would you take? Which would any human being take in his spare time?

Billy taught me that people want to be excited. They want fun. He rubbed that in. For years after the Centennial fairs, whenever he saw me he'd ask, "Want another lesson in show business?"

So I learned that my own tastes weren't necessarily the best guide to what people would buy. I remembered this lesson when I began staging "People Are Funny." Many gags on that show were extravagant slapstick that I didn't personally care for: pies in the face, elephants, banana peels. But I used them because Billy had taught me that people enjoy such stunts. As the show succeeded, Billy began crowing whenever he saw me, "Now you're getting the idea, Art. Now you're catching on." People *are* funny, aren't they?

Isn't there a lesson in this for all salesmen? Don't we all rely too much on our own preferences, our own hunches, instead of trying to find out what our customers prefer? Don't we tend to push a few items in our product line and ignore others that don't appeal to us personally?

The importance of studying the tastes of prospects was proven in one sales exploit by Charles W. Brown, a young salesman who was just starting his own stained glass business in Minneapolis. Brown took a big contract away from the top companies in the business because he thought about the temperament of the buyers. In this case the buyers were western outdoorsmen: cattle ranchers and wheat farmers. But the eastern big-city salesmen soliciting the business tried to sell them "exquisitely beautiful" designs. Brown got the order by offering a "rugged and bold" design, and went on to become president of the Pittsburgh Plate Glass Company.

Billy Rose knew that most of his customers liked everything big and bright and noisy. But there are many different ways to appeal to an audience, or to a business prospect. And as I've said, Billy could be wily in approaching a man through a window when the front door was closed. I remember only one time when his go-betweens proved unable to help him solve a major sales problem by remote control. That time he turned to another clever sales strategy and succeeded again.

Once more it was a problem of getting in to see a man who despised him: Grover Whalen, New York City's famous greeter, politico, and best-dressed man.

Whalen had been appointed president of the World's Fair New York was to stage in 1939. Billy yearned to be put in charge of the Fair's amusement enterprises. But Whalen ignored all hints and nudges from Billy's friends. When Billy peppered him with telegrams and letters and tried to apply for the job in person, Whalen refused to see him and gave the job to someone else.

Undiscouraged, Billy said, "If Grover Whalen won't let me in to see him, I've got to make him come to see me."

He did. On a grand scale he used a technique any salesman can use in smaller ways.

"It cost me fifty grand to meet Whalen under the right auspices," Billy said later, "but I got it all back twentyfold." Billy's first step was to open a cabaret, the Casa Mañana, and then to announce that he would use it to stage an hour-long musical to be called *Let's Play Fair*. He caused word to leak out that the central character would be someone closely resembling Grover Whalen.

How could Whalen help getting curious? He soon telephoned Billy: "I understand you're going to do a show ridiculing me."

Billy was betting no man could stay away from a show in which he was the leading character. It was a safe bet. All salesmen know that putting the prospect in the center of the picture makes a sale much easier. That's why desk salesmen place a full-size mirror on the wall in front of the desk they intend to sell, so the prospect can see himself sitting in splendor at the desk. That's why automobile salesmen make the prospect sit at the wheel of the car or better yet, make him drive it. It's why insurance salesmen give away a notebook with a prospect's own name gold-stamped on it. Any man's eye is caught by his own name, his own face.

Billy made sure of his bet by sending a telegram shortly before *Let's Play Fair* opened: DEAR GROVER I'M SAVING A DOWN FRONT TABLE FOR YOU AND YOUR PARTY ON OPENING NIGHT. COME AND SEE YOURSELF AS OTHERS SEE YOU. KIND REGARDS BILLY.

Whalen and his entourage arrived half an hour before curtain time. The Casa Mañana staff did everything but strew petals in their path. A bucket brigade of waiters kept the table well-supplied with champagne and steak. The show was a handsome tribute to Whalen. The actor who impersonated him was as handsome, graceful, and well-dressed as Whalen himself. When the show was over Mr. World's Fair told Billy, "It's a fine show. We could use something that good at the Fair. Drop into my office tomorrow morning and we'll talk about it."

Just to make sure of clinching the sale, Billy pulled another surprise when he arrived the next morning. He said, "Mr. Whalen, I'd like to show you some pictures of Cleveland."

Cleveland? Why Cleveland? By provoking his prospect's curiosity, Billy got full attention.

Across Whalen's desk he spread a hundred $1,000 bills, each bearing the picture of Grover Cleveland. This would be "a little deposit" for a show he wanted to stage at the Fair, he said. As Billy told me later, "Whalen knew that anyone can write a check that bounces. I wanted him to see with his own eyes that I was solvent."

Whalen let Billy book the 10,000-seat Marine Amphitheatre at the entrance to the Midway. There Billy staged his brilliant water show, the *Aquacade,* which proved the most popular show at the Fair and paid more rent than any other concession. Five million people paid to see it and it netted Billy a clear profit of $1,400,000.

PUT HIM IN THE PLACE OF HONOR

Spotlighting the other fellow is a good way to get his interest, and to put him in a receptive frame of mind. Occasionally it may be the only way to sell a really tough customer. Once it sold the crusty old J. P. Morgan; another time it sold a haughty German general.

Morgan had repeatedly refused to buy the Carnegie Steel Company. Both Andrew Carnegie and Elbert Gary, shrewd salesmen in their own right, had failed to persuade Morgan to make this huge buy. Finally they entrusted Charles Schwab, president of the company, with the task of changing the tycoon's mind.

So what did Schwab do? He arranged a banquet in Morgan's

honor, given by a number of New York bankers who were mutual friends of Schwab and Morgan. (Of course you recognize the same go-between strategy I highlighted earlier.)

Schwab, naturally, was the main speaker at the banquet and Morgan was in the very rare position of having to listen without a chance to say No. Schwab reeled off such impressive facts about the future possibilities of the steel industry that his audience was convinced. Without seeming to address his remarks to Morgan, and without naming any companies specifically, he showed what a thriving organization could be created by a merger of several companies.

When the dinner was over, Morgan sought him out for questioning. Schwab sold the Carnegie steel works for $492 million. This led to the formation of the U.S. Steel Corporation with Schwab himself as president. So Charles Schwab had set up one of the biggest deals in history by his adroitness in capturing J. P. Morgan's attention.

As for the German general, the salesman who sold him an unwelcome idea was none other than Herbert Hoover, who at that time was head of war relief work in German-occupied Belgium early in World War I. The Belgians were near starvation, but the German war machine didn't seem to mind. Infuriated by American newspaper criticism, the Germans determined to take revenge by kicking Hoover and his Commission for Relief out of Belgium.

Hoover rushed to the German Great Headquarters. (America was still neutral at that stage of the war.) A top Prussian officer there raged at him, "Your men are a set of spies! You must all leave Belgium at once!" Hoover's arguments made no impression.

But in this crisis Hoover got an idea. He asked quietly, "What about your place in history, General?"

The general stopped shouting and listened. Hoover had found his sensitive spot. Above all, this proud military man valued his record. It was the center of his ego.

Hoover went on, pointing up the danger to this all-powerful German's reputation as a soldier if he presided over the starvation of a whole nation. He personally, the general with the decisive vote, would be remembered as one of history's cruelest men.

The general blustered but his rage was gone. He told Hoover to come see him tomorrow morning.

Hoover had made his sale. The Belgian relief commission stayed.

Because Hoover stopped to think carefully about the other man's ego he was able to influence him. Such unlike celebrities as Herbert Hoover and Billy Rose had that much in common: They took pains to show a hostile man that they considered him important. Next time we're hunting for a way to change no to yes, let's consider the chances of making the other fellow a star, at least in his own imagination.

And let's not be afraid to show admiration whenever we feel it, as Billy Rose habitually did. How warmly we all respond to the man who shows that he is genuinely glad to see us.

There is much to like and admire in almost anyone. Maybe Billy Rose never read Ralph Waldo Emerson, but I think he knew instinctively what the Yankee essayist and poet had pointed out: "Every man I meet is my superior in some way. In that, I can learn of him."

If that was true of Emerson, isn't it likely to be twice as true of you and me? Let's think less about ourselves and more about our customers.

2 -- HE TOOK NO FOR A STARTER

Selling by Surprise

If you're like most salesmen, you tend to shy away from trying to open new accounts. The brush-off by receptionists, the runaround by underlings, the curt refusal by top men when you finally reach them. Who wants all that grief?

It's so much easier and more pleasant just to service existing accounts and wait for prospects to come to you, and maybe use old customers to help get new ones. But, of course, if you were content in that kind of rut you wouldn't be reading this book, because you'd be a rank-and-file salesman uninterested in reaching for the big, hard sales that bring the big, juicy rewards.

The salesmen whose yearly incomes soar above $25,000 and may pass $100,000 are the kind who woo new business. They are rare and eagerly sought after by employers. In our fast-changing civilization, newness is everywhere: new markets, new ventures, new technology, and new ideas. The marketplace is crowded with new products that jump off the drawing boards and pop out of the Patent Office at the fantastic rate of about 500 every week. Somebody must sell them. And you probably know from your own experience that whatever is new and different is hard to sell. That's why so many psychological tests for selecting salesmen, so many job descriptions, so many evaluation systems, and incentive plans are designed to find and reward men who can lay siege to virgin territory and open prospects' eyes to the value of unfamiliar goods or services.

So let's assume that's what you aim to do.

You're going to solicit a new account, we'll say, in territory where your company and products are unknown. To make it even harder (yet typical enough of today's commerce) we'll say that the products don't even exist yet. Your company can't start making them unless you bring in the orders.

This was the task that repeatedly faced Henry J. Kaiser at crises of his career. His unusual style of salesmanship can work wonders for you too.

Frequently he had to invade America's toughest market— Washington, D.C.—and get huge orders from the government for products he had never built. In his case the problem was especially rugged because he was worse than a stranger; most people are fairly open-minded toward a stranger, but everyone knew that Henry Kaiser had spent his life in the contracting business, building roads and dams. Now he sought to convince Washington that he could build ships, aircraft, and automobiles; could design and operate steel mills, aluminum smelters, and magnesium plants. It was almost as if I, Art Linkletter, should approach you with a proposition that I would make a better wristwatch for you, or produce finer and cheaper rubber than you could get from any existing sources. Knowing how long I'd concentrated on show business, you'd be extremely skeptical, wouldn't you?

But Henry Kaiser was a miraculous salesman as well as a master builder. I watched him at close range during World War II, beginning when he hired me as a broadcaster to talk women into taking hard-hat riveting jobs at his five vast shipyards in Richmond, California. Later we were personal friends. I learned a lot about salesmanship from him. Let's watch him in action and see how his remarkable sales methods can help you.

On one of his first trips to Washington in 1939, he went in search of a $9 million government loan to build a magnesium plant. The likeliest source was the Reconstruction Finance Corporation, a vast labyrinth ruled by a granite-faced Texas banker, Jesse H. Jones. Rather than talk to any subordinates, Kaiser wangled an interview with the top man himself, always the best technique when you're trying to make a big sale because subordinates seldom have authority to okay anything big.

Jones coldly asked Kaiser what experience he'd had with magnesium production. Kaiser, an honest salesman who never tried to fool people, answered, "None."

"Then you won't get a dime from the RFC," Jones said.

Kaiser always took No as a starter, as the normal response. He kept right on talking. Finally, to get rid of him, Jones said he would think it over. Kaiser pressed, "When can we talk again?"

"Call me at my office tonight about nine," Jones said. When Kaiser phoned, Jones was gone. He called Jones's room at the Shoreham Hotel. No answer.

Early next morning Kaiser phoned again. Mr. Jones was sleeping and could not be disturbed. Kaiser phoned every twenty minutes until Jones came on the phone. "I'll see you in the lobby in half an hour," Jones said. But when he came out of the elevator he strode past Kaiser without a flicker of recognition.

What would you have done at that point?

Probably no two supersalesmen would respond identically; they don't fit a pattern because selling is an art rather than a science. Billy Rose's reaction probably would have been to seek powerful friends who could help sell his idea to Jesse Jones. But Henry Kaiser used quite a different tactic. He believed in shock: in capturing people's attention by doing something surprising.

KAISER SURPRISES

So he bustled through the Shoreham's whirling doors just as Jones was stepping into a limousine. Beaming as happily as if he'd been invited, he brushed past the startled chauffeur and scrambled in beside Jones.

Faced with such huge good humor, Jones joined in Kaiser's laughter, and chuckled all the way to the RFC. As he entered his private office with Kaiser beside him, he handed his wallet and watch to his secretary. "Take these before this fellow gets them," he said. He granted Kaiser the loan.

Now, I don't know what Kaiser said during the ride from the hotel to the RFC. But I'm pretty sure it was his manner, rather than any specific argument he advanced, that melted Jones's hostility. Selling is at least 80 percent enthusiasm, and Kaiser was the most enthusiastic man I ever knew. This go-getting, free-swinging, voluble titan believed intensely in each project he tackled; he loved it and never had a moment's doubt he could accomplish it.

There is something psychologists call the law of similar response. It means that people tend to mirror the attitude of anyone talking to them. If he is friendly, they tend to be friendly. If he smiles, they usually smile back. If he shows enthusiasm, they catch it by contagion. This was one great secret of Kaiser's success.

He set the atmosphere of his encounters. It was an atmosphere crackling with excitement and joy, in which no problem seemed too difficult and no task too great. There was nothing synthetic about his mood. He genuinely felt that way. And he wasn't afraid to show his emotions. He didn't worry about dignity. I've seen him leap onto a dragline or a scraper to tell the operators what a grand job they were doing, or just to get a better view of the wonders they performed. At one of my shipyard broadcasts he seized the microphone on impulse and shouted to

Charles Luckman

workers, "I love you all!" Another time he sang into the mike, "Oh what a beautiful morning! Oh what a day to do work!" People almost always warmed to his enthusiasm.

He banked on this law of similar response when he jumped into Jones's limousine. Actually, he wasn't gambling much. He wouldn't have been any worse off than before if Jones had ordered him out of the car.

But his gamble paid off and from then on Jones was on his side. I happened to be in Jones's office one day while Kaiser was describing plans for the new magnesium facility. Kaiser was so breathless with excitement that all his listeners were carried away. We felt as if not a moment could be spared to get this plant built so it could help win the war. Kaiser was setting up a miniature model of the plant (models were great sales aids for him, an important point I'll discuss in a moment) and as his hands were busy with the cardboard, words were tumbling from his lips: "Now there's an important point I want to show you on the blueprints—where are the blueprints? Oh, they're in my briefcase! It's in the office down the hall. Say, Jesse, while I'm setting this up could you get that briefcase for me?"

Without thinking twice, Jones hustled down the corridor for Kaiser's briefcase. I wouldn't have believed it if I hadn't seen it. One of the capital's most powerful and prominent bureaucrats, a man who was to be Secretary of Commerce and prominently mentioned as a possible Vice President, was running an errand for the brash upstart from California. Jones seldom smiled or showed emotion but his actions proved how warmly he felt toward Kaiser.

Probably the toughest crew of prospects Kaiser ever tackled were the top admirals of the U.S. Navy. In 1942, when Nazi Germany was sinking the free world's ships faster than they were built, Kaiser conceived a baby aircraft carrier that might be mass-produced in five days. (At that time the fastest ship-yards were averaging 253 days per ship.) He got the Maritime

Commission to okay his idea. Now who would sell the Navy on it? Kaiser would.

Admiral Ernest King, the nation's highest admiral, was away when Kaiser hit Washington one hot June day. Rather than wait, Kaiser insisted on seeing the number two man, Vice Admiral Horne, and the Under Secretary of the Navy, James Forrestal. They weren't interested. Nevertheless he got a hearing from a board of sixteen admirals. "Okay this ship, and we'll lick the submarines," Kaiser told them excitedly.

What an insult to decades of naval lore, science, and experience. Who did this civilian landlubber think he was, trying to sell the Navy a design for ships? The admirals voted 16–0 against his plan, as Kaiser probably expected. He knew that few new accounts are opened on the first try. He didn't slow down. For several days he prodded the top men of the Maritime Commission and the War Production Board, the White House secretaries, and others. Then Admiral King got back to Washington, but refused to see Kaiser.

So Kaiser, knowing that King often lunched at the Army and Navy Club, lay in wait for him there. When King swept through the lobby with his aides, Kaiser buttonholed him and began explaining his plan. According to one spectator, King shot him an icy look, told him in a four-letter word what his plan consisted of, and pushed past.

This was a time for dynamite, Kaiser decided. He caught the admiral's shoulder, spun him around, and continued talking. King said, "Take your blank-blank hand off me." There might have been punches thrown had not other officers intervened. The story was all over Washington by nightfall.

Would you have bet, at this point, that the Navy would ever buy anything from Henry Kaiser?

But Kaiser's tactics were coolly calculated. He realized what his basic problem was: The gold braid would simply ignore a ship design from a newcomer who admittedly had made his reputation as a gravel contractor and dam builder. Therefore he set out to make the admirals mad enough to stop ignoring him.

Now he got presidential secretary Marvin McIntyre to submit his plan on one sheet of paper to President Roosevelt, who scribbled across it, "I'll take one hundred." So the unfriendly admirals had to listen. When Kaiser met with them again, he brought along three-dimensional cardboard models that they could fit together, to *see* and *feel* how easily the ship would be put together, instead of trying to visualize it from his sales talk. The gold braid gradually warmed up and eventually became pro-Kaiser.

MAGIC IN MODELS

The eye remembers what the ear forgets. So does the hand. This is why Kaiser, in selling new products that existed only in his imagination, handed out models whenever he could. A realtor used the same approach to sell a vacant factory. He made up a plaster of Paris model of the building and put it in a cardboard box with fallaway covers. When the covers fell outward they made a diagram of the streets around the site. He sent 300 of these models to prospective buyers and sold the plant in one day.

Likewise, Allis-Chalmers' model-toting salesmen carried miniature transformers and twenty-seven other tiny replicas of equipment. When set up on specially ruled layout pads, the equipment formed an exact scale model of power distribution as it might be in the prospect's own plant. Busy executives often got fascinated and stole the show from Chalmers' salesmen, happily building their own orders.

In the years when refrigerators were new, salesmen got orders by calling on housewives with a large sheet of paper printed with spaces corresponding to the shelf areas of the refrigerator. They spread the paper on a kitchen table and asked the lady to put the contents of her present icebox onto the diagram. Thus she discovered for herself how much extra space the refrigerator would give her.

It's good salesmanship to get prospects *doing* something with you instead of just listening. Insurance salesmen hand a pen to a prospect and ask him, "Will you write these figures down as I give them to you?" This holds his interest. Later when they're ready to try to close, they hand him an order blank already filled in as fully as possible, with a bright mark penciled where he should sign, and say, "Is this right? Will you write your name here, the same as I've typed it in up at the top?"

Similarly, hardware merchants sell more hammers by pointing the handles toward the customers so that he feels an impulse to grasp one. A textile salesman carries a little magnifying glass and invites prospects to peer at the fabric.

Once I was able to help a Girl Scout speed up her door-to-door sale of cookies. I suggested how she could get her prospects involved: "When someone comes to the door, offer one of the cookies and say 'Here, won't you taste one? Don't they taste good?' " She soon sold out her whole allotment.

Henry Kaiser started his magnificent business rise as a salesman. He left school at thirteen to work for $1.50 a week as cash boy in a dry goods store, but seized every chance to wait on customers too. This gave him confidence in meeting people, so he soon set forth on his own as an itinerant photographer. At Lake Placid he saw opportunity in the throngs of tourists. He said to W. W. Brownell, who owned a photographic shop there, "If I triple your business in a year, will you give me a half interest in the store?" Brownell chuckled but agreed. A year later Kaiser was half owner.

In 1906 he went West in search of bigger opportunities. He ran out of money in Spokane, applied for work at a big hardware firm, and "hounded one man so persistently that he nearly threw me out," as Kaiser later recalled. The company had no jobs open. But Kaiser noticed a group of girls unpacking and cleaning silverware and began helping them. Soon a supervisor told James McGowan, the owner of the hardware firm: "There's a fellow in there who's a live wire and seems to know what it's all about. Let's put him in charge."

So Kaiser had a job at seven dollars a week. He soon became a salesman for McGowan. Along with frying pans and fishing tackle, he sold structural steel. He called on contractors and found the best way to make them listen was to give them a hand with their work. If they were on the job at 4:00 A.M. or 10:00 P.M. he was there. He soon landed a $10,000 order for steel in Spokane's Monroe Street bridge.

THE SMILE THAT WINS

His beaming smile and hearty enthusiasm kept him moving up, selling his way into bigger and bigger contracts. This in spite of the fact that he often had little to smile about. His father had died young, leaving him to support a widowed mother who eventually died because he couldn't afford adequate medical care for her. Later his wife fell seriously ill and hospital bills put him deep in debt. Later still, when he became a contractor, he lost everything by underestimating his costs on a road-building job.

But Kaiser didn't believe in failure. One day when the oil tanker *Schenectady* cracked open at his Swan Island shipyard, he just said "All right," when he got the news. He went on, "You see, Art, we'll learn a lot from that accident. We'll build better boats because it happened. We make progress by such disasters." Why shouldn't we all face setbacks with that spirit? If we do, we can be star salesmen.

Kaiser always had a warm happy smile for people around him. Do you ever notice how often the smiling man gets the breaks, and the glum-looking man is shunned? The ancient Chinese had a wise proverb, "A man without a smiling face must not open a shop." A lifeless attitude kills sales. A genuine smile is an easy way to start a sale.

A young man named Sam Vauclain once found his normal smile was worth $40,000. He was asked to put up a bond for this amount when he was only a lathe operator. He couldn't afford it. To his amazement, a Jewish tailor named Sheeline, whom he barely knew, offered to go his bond. Sam accepted and asked why he was willing to risk the money. Sheeline said, "Because you're one of the few people in town who bother to greet me pleasantly on the street." Sam kept smiling throughout his life, and became president of the Baldwin Locomotive Works.

Probably both he and Henry Kaiser had to force themselves to smile sometimes. But I'm sure they learned early that by acting enthusiastic they could *become* enthusiastic, a strange truth about human nature that every salesman needs to keep constantly in mind.

Fired up with enthusiasm, you are ready to tackle the toughest sales problems. You can charge, smiling, into new territories and win new customers. It was an article of faith with Harry Kaiser that a man grows by tackling strange new jobs, and that unfamiliarity with them is an asset rather than a handicap. He electrified people around him with that same faith. Clay Bedford shovelled sand in one of Kaiser's first construction gangs, ran the garages at the Hoover Dam job, and got a call from Kaiser in 1940: "I've just signed a contract to build ships and you're going to build them." Two years later Bedford was bossing 92,000 people and running four shipyards. George Havas was a Kaiser engineer on a Cuban sugar plantation; Kaiser put him to work building roads, then phoned him one night in 1942: "Go out and build a steel plant. What kind? Why, just a steel plant! Pick a site and get started."

Dusty Rhoades caught Kaiser's eye as a gravel inspector in 1927. In twelve years he was running the world's biggest cement plant; in 1946 he got a call from Henry: "We're moving into the aluminum business and you're going to run it." Gene Trefethen was driving a gravel pit dinky at Livermore when Kaiser spotted him. He went to Harvard's business school, then travelled with Henry as his secretary, took over administrative tasks, and was awakened one morning by Kaiser pounding on his bedroom door shouting, "Get up! You're going to manufacture automobiles!" Trefethen eventually became the money man for all the fifty-five Kaiser companies in twenty-one countries.

During the war, their we-can-do-anything spirit enabled Henry Kaiser and his men to blitz Washington for $227,500,000 in federal loans to start new enterprises. He repaid it all, plus $39 million interest, a full twenty-five years ahead of schedule. The Navy put his ships to such good use that Winston Churchill later wrote Kaiser, "Your escort carriers turned the tide of the submarine war."

Whenever people said No to his sales talk—which happened often, as I've said, because he was opening new accounts all his life—he cast about for some way to shake them up. If he couldn't do it jovially, as he did with Jesse Jones and Admiral King, as a last resort he might startle them with sheer rage.

SHOCK TREATMENTS

I remember he once addressed a big meeting of the Associated General Contractors, which had elected him president but ignored the ideas he advocated. At that meeting he stormed and ranted. Veins swelled in his neck. His massive body shook. Many of us in the audience seriously feared he might drop dead of apoplexy. But during a recess I met him in the washroom. He was as calm as the Pacific on a quiet day. "How'm I doing?" he asked me. His seeming anger was only an act.

Real anger is a luxury salesmen can't afford. Like everyone else, if they get mad they make mistakes. But some of the great salesmen know when a pretense of justifiable anger can get results.

Frank Davis, the insurance salesman who rose to the top of Equitable Life's eight thousand agents, once made an appointment to see an important prospect. He arrived punctually but was kept waiting in the corridor. After a while the executive strolled out. "What can I do for you?" he snapped. "Make it brief."

"I can't talk standing up," Davis said, "and I don't intend to try. I have a definite appointment with you. If you want to keep your word and listen to the kind of service we can give you, I'm at your service. Otherwise I'll say goodby right now."

The startled executive stared a moment, then held out his hand. "You're right, my friend. Come inside."

A few minutes later Davis signed up the prospect for $50,000 worth of insurance. His carefully aimed outburst of temper, against a man who had imposed on him and was bound to feel secretly ashamed, had gotten the attention he needed.

It is a principle of psychology that people tend to value you at just about the same level as you value yourself. "Every man stamps his value on himself," wrote the philosopher Friedrich von Schiller. The able man rises above petty slights from others. But if and when naysayers clearly put themselves in the wrong on a vital ethical issue, he decides first of all whether fighting of any kind is the right strategy. And if it is, he chooses the likeliest method of attack, which may range from such a simple and direct rebuke as Frank Davis used to the frightening rage of Henry Kaiser at the contractors' meeting.

When Charles G. Dawes, who was later to become Ambassador to England and Vice President of the United States, was only a lieutenant colonel during World War I, General John J. Pershing (head of American forces in Europe) sent him to negotiate with a British military mightiness in London. That exalted general froze Dawes with a glance, demanding, "Where is General Pershing? General Pershing should be here."

"I'm here!" barked Dawes. "I represent General Pershing. I'm here with all his power, God damn you!"

Was Dawes shot for insubordination? Far from it. The startled dignitary quickly sat down to work out an agreement with him, and later not only recommended him for a distinguished British decoration, but crossed the Atlantic just to attend a banquet in his honor.

It is risky to insist that your own importance be recognized. The only time to do it is when the other fellow has put himself completely in the wrong and left himself without a comeback; when you must fight not only to maintain your own self-respect, but also to hold the respect of others. People respect a man who keeps his integrity, although they laugh at a touchy egotist who frets about his rank and privileges.

When we surprise a prospect by putting up a fight, in order to win we must be able to answer yes to these questions: Do we have something to offer that meets a need? Are we sincere in urging it on the prospect for his own good? Is our real purpose not to tell somebody off, but to win a friendly response from the people who really count? And is fighting the best way to get it?

In ninety-nine of every one hundred cases, you can capture an unfriendly prospect's attention with less drastic surprise. I knew one insurance salesman who startled his prospect by snapping a pencil in two. He threw it away and told the suddenly attentive listener, "Arithmetic and figuring can't support your wife! If you die tomorrow, only one thing can take care of her. That's insurance."

Frank Bettger, once a third baseman for the St. Louis Cardinals and later a fabulously successful insurance man, often told lecture audiences how he made a $250,000 sale in fifteen minutes against a dozen competitors. The prospect had a stack of proposals on his desk when Bettger got in to see him. He said, "Mr. Bettger, if you want to submit a proposition, make up figures for $250,000 of insurance and mail it to me. I'll study it with the other proposals. If your plan is the cheapest and best, you'll get the account."

Bettger countered by saying the unexpected: "Knowing what

I do about the insurance business, if you were my own brother, I'd tell you to take all those proposals and throw them into the wastepaper basket."

The startled prospect looked up. Bettger went on to explain that only an actuary could evaluate the plans adequately, and that in all probability they were much alike; that during the weeks spent studying them, many things might happen that could make the prospect uninsurable—and so on through a successful (and carefully planned) sales talk that Bettger wouldn't have been permitted to give if he hadn't shocked his listener at the outset.

Ivy Lee, the great public relations counselor, once went to England to try to persuade Lady Astor to lay the cornerstone of the new Waldorf Astoria Hotel. She refused abruptly. "It would not be dignified. You merely wish me to advertise your hotel."

Instead of arguing and getting nowhere, Lee sprang a surprise by agreeing with her. "That's perfectly true," he said.

So now she was listening. He went on, "However, you too want certain things. You want to reach the public with certain ideas. You'll be on a nationwide broadcast at the cornerstone ceremony." He went on to explain that she needn't praise the hotel; only her presence was requested. He soon won her over. But if he hadn't surprised her at the start, conceding she was right about an objection that she considered basic and final, she would have cut short his plea and terminated the interview.

THEY LISTEN WHEN THEY'RE CURIOUS

Farmers are notably cool to strange salesmen. But one bond salesman signed them up wherever he went, after using surprise to get them in a listening mood. He would approach a farmer in the barn and merely stand watching the cows for five minutes, which perplexed the laconic farmer. Then the salesman would ask, "How would you like to get a cow like this free every year?"

Naturally the farmer listened while the salesman explained that by taking money from the bank and putting it into bonds, the interest would buy a cow a year.

Any salesman can find legitimate ways to surprise a prospect. Bill Rudge, a salesman of fine printing, used to send ahead two little page boys in bright uniforms. They arrived at the prospect's office a half hour ahead of Rudge, and set up huge samples on chairs and desks. So when Rudge arrived the prospect was already thinking about him and wondering what would happen next.

The busy president of a big advertising agency refused to see salesmen. But one ingenious fellow got to him by phoning the president's secretary and saying, "Will you ask your boss whether the agency could handle more business, or whether you're at capacity now?" What adman could resist that question? The president took the telephone and litsened carefully to the salesman for a minute. Then he gave the salesman an appointment, and finally bought the service being offered.

Surprise works on clerks as well as on presidents and admirals. In Dallas, an ice cream company put over a new milk drink by instructing its salesmen to go to a soda fountain and tell the clerk, "Make me a milk shake." Naturally the clerk would ask what flavor. "No flavor," the salesman would answer. "Just shake it up. I don't want any flavor in it—yet."

As the mixer began to whir, the salesman would produce an envelope, hand it to the puzzled clerk, and tell him, "Mix this in it."

"What is it?" the clerk always asked. The salesman retorted, "What do you care? I'm buying the shake. Can't I put whatever I want in it?"

The salesman would sip the drink with obvious delight while the clerk watched. In leaving, the salesman would toss the clerk a couple of the envelopes and say, "Make yourself one."

You know what happened. Nothing could stop that clerk from shaking up that drink and tasting it. It tasted good, so the clerk would tell his ice cream supplier: "Say, I just drank a new drink and it's good."

On being asked for particulars, he would explain, "Some guy was in here and handed me a sample. Do you have it?" Whereupon the wily ice cream supplier would respond, "Sure we have it. We sent that man in to see you. How many can you use this week?"

A salesman of industrial products used a walnut shell as his bombshell. He sold a long line. Like most long-line salesmen, he had a bulky catalogue and a huge sample case. A big portfolio and catalogue are two reasons why most buyers try to dodge a long-line salesman; they're afraid he'll take an hour showing his wares. But this salesman disarmed them at the start.

"We handle more than two thousand items," he admitted with a friendly grin, "but the reason you should deal with us is so simple that we put it in a nutshell." As he said this he pressed a walnut into the prospect's hand.

Opening the shell, the prospect found a ticker tape that read: "More items from one source—and from the most convenient warehouse." Since purchasing agents have to buy hundreds of items, this was enough to catch their attention. And the salesman went on to build his story.

Surprise. Enthusiasm. Persistence. These are tools the star salesman uses to help him open up new markets.

He knows that the closed door, the screen of secretaries, the No is normal. He expects them. When you meet that common ordinary No your work begins. Find a way around it, over it, or under it—and if your search reveals no way, just invent some dynamite.

It helps to have firm faith in yourself and in God. This was part of what Henry Kaiser taught me. Some of his friends were inclined to quit struggling and rely on prayer when they met difficulty. He used to tell them a story about two boys who were hurrying to school and were afraid they would be late. They'd both had religious upbringing.

"Let's stop and pray," said one. The other replied, "No, let's run and pray."

It was one of Kaiser's favorite little stories. He was a religious man. And he believed that we should look to God for help but do our level best meanwhile. Try it the next time you need a way to win a new customer.

3 -- THE PERILS OF OVERPERSUADING

High Pressure versus Helpfulness

Late one afternoon I was hurrying to get ready to leave when my secretary said, "A Mr. Walsh claims it's very important that you see him for five minutes. He won't say why. He won't say whom he represents. He just insists it's no ordinary business call."

"If he wants to sell me something, he'd better come some other day," I said. "I'm too rushed to consider any sales proposition today."

She relayed this word. Mr. Walsh still pressed for five minutes of my time. I sighed, "Okay, send him in."

He strode in smiling, and in one smooth motion pulled a chair beside my desk, opened a briefcase, and produced a pad and pen. Meanwhile he was saying, "I understand you're going away, Mr. Linkletter. You'll only need a few minutes to tell me what I want to know. And by the time you return I'll have exciting news for you."

It was a well-rehearsed entrance. Being a salesman myself, I was impressed by his ingenuity. He'd gotten past a receptionist and a secretary, seated himself beside me, secured my undivided attention, and started a sales pitch. Still I didn't feel friendly.

PRESSURE CAN BACKFIRE

"Mr. Walsh, you haven't said who you are or what you're selling," I said. "You know that you broke in on me when I'm very busy. So your next words had better be good. What is it you want?"

"Just a list of the stocks you own. Under the circumstances a partial list will do. No amounts, just the names of the companies. By the time you're back, I'll be able to advise switches—."

"So you're a stockbroker's salesman."

"Oh no, Mr. Linkletter." He thrust a sales brochure into my hand. "We provide special investment counselling—."

"Hold it right there. You gave me a clever rush act. But I don't like to be high-pressured. I bet you don't either. Anyhow I'll have to pressure you right out of my office, right now, so I can catch my plane." The salesman had forever lost any chance to sell me, because he made the fatal mistake of pressing for an interview at the wrong time.

I suppose his tricky way of getting into a prospect's office enabled him to make some sales. But I'm sure he lost others because he didn't have enough consideration for the prospect to distinguish between the right and wrong times to make his approach. His short-range goal of getting through the door spoiled his long-range aim of building a clientele. A lot of prospects undoubtedly felt resentful and refused to buy.

TIMING TAKES TACT

Smart salesmen, like smart basketball players, don't shoot every time they get the ball. They work into scoring position first. A noted business psychologist, Dr. Donald Laird, used to say that of all qualities which make a salesman succeed the most important is tact. A tactful salesman avoids irritating people. He can judge when to try for a score, when to play for time.

Some salesmen never learn tact. They waste years trying to trick or bulldoze people into buying. I remember a man I met at the San Diego YMCA when I worked there as a young man. He was middle-aged, but he came to practice boxing. Once I asked why he chose such strenuous recreation.

"I need it in my business, to defend myself," he said.

I whistled. "You must be in a rough line of work."

"I am. I'm a salesman."

Fascinated, I got him to explain that customers frequently insulted him, so he had to fight now and then. You can imagine that he never sold much.

He was an extreme case. There are many lesser examples. We've all known so-called salesmen who flared up, "How can I make a living if you won't buy from me?" Or who stuck a foot in the door. Or who clung to a prospect's arm. In the long run they don't succeed. They never can go back for repeat orders that bring the quick profits.

To love our neighbors happens to be an aid to successful selling. The old-fashioned salesman who regarded people merely as stepping-stones to his own profit would never build a permanent clientele because a key ingredient in effortless selling, the spirit of service, was lacking.

THE GODFREY TREATMENT

Arthur Godfrey has been the very opposite of a high-pressure seller, so much so that he's almost caused heart attacks among makers of some products he was supposed to be plugging.

This red-headed ex-sailor has been my "opposite number" during my forty years in broadcasting. When I was learning the tricks of the microphone trade in San Diego, he was the early morning broadcaster for a station in Washington, D.C. Years later we were running mates for Pillsbury, teaming up to broadcast its first bakeoff from the grand ballroom of the Waldorf-Astoria. Arthur and I have traded quips on each other's programs and met at many world premieres, state fairs and banquets. I like him. I admire his unique persuasive ability. His style is completely different from mine, but the results are much the same: We convince the average person we are telling the truth.

Godfrey's trademark has been his folksy, friendly, easy-going way of talking. He refuses to get excited about what he's describing. He is amused and unflustered, with a calm air of authority underneath it all. Unhurried, colloquial, even ungrammatical at times, he gives listeners the feeling that here is an unpretentious neighbor dropping in to exchange gossip and pass along a few tips. Listening to a typical Godfrey show is like eavesdropping on a party line.

Often he seems to be kidding his sponsors. The chuckle in his voice lets you know he doesn't take himself or his wares too seriously. There's none of the listen-damn-you manner so common on the air. Yet his sincerity and knowledgeableness keep you listening.

He started all this in his first wakeup shows in Washington, tweaking the pompous claims that were handed him to read. "Marvelous fur coat for $115," he would read, then snort in disgust, "Imagine anyone dumb enough to believe it's mink for that kind of dough. It's probably dyed rabbit."

While the sponsor and station bigwigs were picking themselves off the floor, Arthur continued, "But where in the world are you gonna get better dyed rabbit than at Hamilton's Fur Store? Those coats would probably fool a real mink for a while. And of course it's gotta be a bargain for only $115."

Before they could get to the phone to fire him, the bosses found that customers were flocking in to buy the furs. His kind of selling had riveted listeners' attention because it was so different. He had made fun of the commercial as an obvious

Henry J. Kaiser

exaggeration. This convinced his audience that he was honest and independent. Then he followed with a frank, believable analysis of how good the offer really was.

It's a clever selling strategy. In later years, with a coast-to-coast following and an astronomical income, Arthur Godfrey proved that it works for many kinds of products.

THE MAKING OF A SOAP SALESMAN

Now let's consider the remarkable techniques of another good friend of mine, Charles Luckman of Los Angeles. His rise and fall—and his second rise, for keeps—illustrate some uses and some misuses of persuasiveness.

About forty years ago, Chuck was walking the streets of Chicago with three brand-new but desperately non-negotiable documents: a college diploma, an architect's license, and a marriage license. He was the son of a clothing salesman, and had been working part-time since he was nine years old: newsboy in the afternoons, jerking sodas at night, delivering groceries on Saturday. He had worked his way through the University of Illinois. But he found there was no work for new architects in that depression summer of 1931.

Finally Chuck got a draftsman's job at $125 a month with Colgate-Palmolive-Peet. One of his first assignments was to lay out a brochure for Palmolive soap. After a look at Chuck's finished layout, the boss growled, "That won't sell soap or anything else."

The slight, intense young man startled the boss by asking, "Can I test it myself? I'll be glad to try it on a few stores."

Maybe Chuck startled himself too by such a proposal. He had no training in salesmanship. But he was accustomed to trying anything and giving it all he had. Moreover, throughout his boyhood he'd noticed that his personality pleased and disarmed people, that they tended to believe whatever he said. (Years later, when he got to the top, this asset would almost ruin him, as we'll see.)

He took his brochure to Chicago's tough South Side. "I figured that if I couldn't sell soap in a dirty slum area, I might as well quit," he told me long afterward. Thus began his transformation into the most successful soap salesman of his generation.

The first storekeeper he approached snarled, "I don't need soap."

Smiling, Chuck responded, "I know you don't. That's why I came to see you. If you needed soap you'd pick up your phone and order some. I'm here to find out *why* you don't need soap. Aren't your customers buying?"

THE IMPORTANCE OF ASKING WHY

It was a flash of inspiration. Maybe the most important word in selling is "why." It should be used more often.

Instead of asking why, many salesmen counter an objection with "yes but," and thereby kill the sale. A salesman gets nowhere by debating. A debate is a contest and who likes to lose a contest?

On the other hand, a friendly "why" can set a favorable mood, two men talking together in a relaxed way.

If your prospect is a real businessman, he likes his business and enjoys talking about it. Your interest in his problem creates a feeling of fellowship. If you find a way to help him, you gain his confidence and respect, which eventually will lead to orders.

Abraham Lincoln said, "If you would win a man to your cause you must first convince him that you are his sincere friend." Isn't this true in all kinds of persuasion?

It was what Luckman was doing. He listened sympathetically to the storekeeper's lament: business was bad, customers weren't buying, nobody had money, and so on. The talk turned (not without some steering by Chuck) to ways of rearranging goods so they would catch customers' eyes.

Chuck peeled off his coat. "Here, I'll help you. Why don't we put the candy bars and cigarettes over there, where people can see them but can't get to them quite so quickly? Lots of people come just for candy or cigarettes, right? If we lead them past these other displays, something may catch their eyes, and they'll want it too."

Finally he got around to soap. "Everyone buys soap now and then. They'll buy it here if they think of it here. So let's not bury it out of sight. We can stack it on this counter nose-high, so they smell that nice clean odor. Notice how good this soap smells."

He handed the storekeeper a bar. He was bringing into play a couple of other proven sales techniques: Get propects doing something with you instead of just listening (as we mentioned in Chapter 2) and appeal to as many of their senses as possible.

Chuck and his prospect built a soap pyramid on the counter —using Chuck's sales brochure as a guide, for this was one of the display techniques shown there. The merchant kept the brochure for future use, thanked Chuck for his help, and as an afterthought ordered more soap since his whole supply was now stacked on display. "Better not order quite that much," Chuck advised him. "We don't want you overstocked."

He was building up welcome for the callback. By similar helpfulness, Chuck and his brochure sold soap in seven of the first eight stores he visited. Maybe by instinct or intuition—but partly, I'm sure, by genuine interest in the storekeepers he visited—Chuck had become a successful salesman overnight. Colgate-Palmolive-Peet pulled him off the drawing board and appointed him citywide troubleshooter for sales problems.

He was sent into sectors of Chicago where little English was spoken. The Poles and Germans and Slavs were charmed by his improvised sign language, his schemes for improving the sales of products other than soap, and his incredible refusals to overstock stores with his wares. At twenty-four he became

CPP's district manager in Milwaukee, where he turned $80,000 of red ink into a profit in one year. This led to a job running CPP's biggest district, six populous Midwestern states, with seventy salesmen. Such a young man in such a big sales job was phenomenal.

HELPFUL SELLING

Chuck trained his salesmen to concentrate on helping dealers, not on selling soap: suggesting attractive displays, new products to carry, improvements in store layout. Winning good will was their objective. High pressure was taboo. But soap orders began to mount.

Pepsodent heard about it and hired Chuck as sales promotion manager at $10,000 a year, which was a high salary in 1936. For fifty-one of his first fifty-two weeks with Pepsodent he was on the road, visiting drugstores and grocery stores, selling the men who sold Pepsodent to the public. By 1942 Pepsodent led the dentifrice field, and by 1943 Chuck was president of Pepsodent.

He rose so fast because he was so different from typical salesmen of that era. To be successful, as they saw it, a man had to be a hustler, a specialist in fooling people. "Let the buyer beware," the old rule handed down from Roman common law, was the byword in that Depression era of flashy hit-and-run salesmanship.

So buyers did learn to beware. Better Business Bureaus sprang up. The Federal Trade Commission cracked down on deceptive advertising and selling.

My point is that Chuck was ahead of his time. There was nothing dazzling about his way of selling. He dressed quietly and spoke quietly. By helping his customers instead of tricking them, he won their confidence and built a steady business of repeat sales.

SIDEWALK SCHOOLS

To help customers, a salesman (or a company) must understand their problems. Therefore, as president of ·Pepsodent, Chuck required all executives to spend a third of their time in the field calling on dealers.

In doing so they uncovered an important principle: in selling low-cost competitive items, a very simple sales message works best. Pepsodent salesmen could tick off perhaps a dozen selling points for their toothpaste. But they found it sold better when they cut their selling message down to just three words: "Makes teeth brighter." So they ignored other points and hammered on that one. (Sometimes a one-point sales talk can also sell complex high-priced assortments. Remember the walnut shell in Chapter 2?)

Pepsodent also discovered the value of making full use of its advertising. Its salesmen carried proofs of Pepsodent magazine and newspaper ads which they spread before storekeepers saying, "See what we do to help you sell Pepsodent? We create consumer demand."

Later, when Pepsodent sponsored Bob Hope's show, the salesmen mentioned this every time they chatted with a dealer. I often wonder why so many of today's salesmen for advertised products never tell dealers about the advertising. Most storekeepers are only half aware, at best, of a TV campaign or print ads that create demand for a product. If reminded, they'd be likely to put that product up front where the demand could pull it across the counter.

Pepsodent became such a sensation that Lever Bros. bought the company in 1944. Lever, a British-owned corporation, has long been one of the world's heaviest advertisers, spending tens of millions yearly.

The talk in the trade was that Lever Bros. bought Pepsodent

partly to get Luckman. He charmed the British directors out of their armchairs by his eagerness to listen to them and seek their opinions. In 1946 they made him president of Lever Bros.

And so at age thirty-seven, Chuck Luckman was the jet-propelled wonder boy of U.S. salesmanship. In fifteen years he had climbed from nowhere to the presidency of a corporate colossus. But with 20-20 hindsight we can see that he unwittingly oversold himself.

WHY LUCKMAN LOST OUT

Salesmen tend to be good mixers, optimists, and dream merchants. If they were pessimists they couldn't sell. But the traits that make a great salesman are likely to make an erratic chief executive. To run a corporation a man needs a strong streak of caution. I know of several enterprises that lost big money by putting a top salesman in charge.

For a while everything seemed rosy at Lever Bros. Knowing that soap can't be sold by advertising alone, Chuck stressed the face-to-face selling that had made his fortune. On his first visit to Los Angeles, he spent a day ringing forty-two doorbells. "I'm a salesman making a survey to find out what housewives think of various soaps," he said. "Which laundry soap do you prefer? Why?" He picked up valuable pointers about his own products and about the competition, which a truly smart persuader studies as keenly as he does his own wares. Chuck sent Lever Bros. vice-presidents onto the streets to find new ways of helping dealers.

He got along as smoothly with nationwide chain executives as he did with neighborhood grocers. He became a friend of President Roosevelt. Maybe he began to feel there was nothing on earth he couldn't master. He took time off to serve the White

House on special assignments. He gave speeches on questions of national policy. He let press agents portray him as an industrial statesman.

But the acclaim worked against him. Now that everyone knew him as the wonder boy, their guard automatically went up. Subconsciously they thought, "Let's see if this whiz kid can overwhelm me."

His decision to move the company's historic headquarters from Boston to New York made him no friends among the Lever nabobs whose homes and friends were anchored in Massachusetts. The "glass skyscraper" he brought into existence on Park Avenue for the new American headquarters caused further confrontations (although it began an entirely new trend in profitless first-floor entranceways to New York office buildings). And finally he fought a losing battle to put Lever into the detergent business in spite of its worldwide domination of the soapmaking industry.

Within the company, Chuck was unconsciously stepping on unseen toes. People were quitting for reasons he knew nothing about. A Lever Bros. Alumni Association grew up to bad-mouth him and the company.

He thought he was doing fine. How could it be otherwise when he was up daily at 5:30 to tackle his briefcase full of papers? When he was the first man to arrive at the office and the last to leave? With his sunny view of life and industry, Chuck assumed that his long days and hard work would keep him on top.

In January 1950 the British heads of Unilever, which owned Lever Bros., sent word they were coming to New York to confer with him. He made no special preparations, assuming it would be a routine meeting. But when the Englishmen arrived, they threw him off balance with questions and complaints. After two days of continuous grilling, he found himself out of a job at age forty.

COMEBACK OF A SUPERSALESMAN

An ex-president of a vast company, departing under a cloud, can't easily step onto a comparable throne elsewhere. Chuck didn't even try. But he didn't drop into limbo either. Instead he planned how to sell himself in a field where salesmanship was almost unknown.

He entered architecture, the profession he'd studied in college but had never practiced. Also he made a resolution never again would he be caught unprepared. He'd always done his homework as a salesman; he would be equally forearmed as an architect. Whenever he went into a meeting with prospective clients, he would be ready with answers for any objection they might raise.

While studying for a California architect's license, he was evaluating himself as a new product to be sold, and sizing up the market for that product. Why should anyone want Charles Luckman to design a building? What could he offer that competitors couldn't?

To meet the objection of his lack of experience, he realized that he would need an experienced architect as partner. So he joined forces with a former college classmate, William L. Pereira, whose small firm had gathered a solid clientele in Los Angeles. Bill would do the designing while Chuck drummed up business, at least for a while.

A NEW SERVICE "FOR SALE"

This still left the question of what Pereira & Luckman could do for customers that other architects couldn't or didn't. The partners decided that their "product" could be augmented. Cost control would be its strong point. Having been a client of architects during his years as a corporate president, Chuck remembered construction often proved more costly than designers had estimated. If he could convince prospects that he knew how to keep costs within estimates, he would have a powerful sales talk.

So he and Pereira added experts whose sole job was to scan every change order during design and construction. If it would add to the cost, the client must be told exactly how much and must okay the change. The P & L designers chafed at this curb on their creativity, but Luckman sold them the idea that even greater art was needed to design the right building within tight cost constraints.

Advertising is considered unethical in the architectural profession. So Luckman had to do the whole selling job, from first approach to final contract-signing, without the massive promotion campaigns that help sell soap and toothpaste.

He jammed his sixty-five-hour weeks with personal calls on prospects, as he had at Pepsodent. And he kept reminding people of his simple sales message: "I was a client and I was building. I grew up with the problems our clients face. That's why we have a cost control system, and it works."

He sold to businessmen because he knew from experience and instinct what businessmen wanted. Selling to the government and to great nonprofit institutions was harder, but by close study he came to see that they would prefer buildings that could be easily changed to meet changing needs. By offering flexible plans he landed big contracts.

"We'll put up a building that can stand alone or can take on new wings harmoniously," he told universities, hospitals, and air-base managers. "If you run low on money, nobody need know."

In less than eight years P & L designed $850 million worth of buildings. Then Pereira sold out to his partner and set up a smaller firm of his own to concentrate on fewer projects while doing more city planning, which he had grown to love. Chuck went on alone to design $1.7 billion worth of construction, making his architectural firm one of America's five biggest.

His genius for self-promotion is muted now. You seldom read much about Chuck Luckman the supersalesman. He has quietly helped form a vast new enterprise that doesn't even bear his name: Ogden Development Corporation. It plans billion-dollar realty projects all over the country. Chuck has proven that architecture can be a business as well as an art. And in these past forty years he has learned, the hard way, lessons in persuasion that we all can use to advantage.

4 -- *ARE YOU LISTENING?*

Persuading by Paying Attention

Winston Churchill used to tell how one word disrupted a top-level meeting of British and American leaders. The British brought in a report on a key matter they had agreed to investigate, and then they proposed to "table it." The Americans reddened and argued against tabling. Bristling at their tone of voice, the British curtly insisted.

The dispute went on for many minutes before someone realized that everybody really agreed. To the British "tabling" meant discussing a matter around the table immediately. To the Americans, tabling meant postponing or shelving. Neither side had really listened. They just reacted to scowls and snarls. They forgot that words mean different things to different people.

Such foul-ups have caused trouble ever since the Old Testament complained, "They have ears and hear not." At times anybody is likely to think, mistakenly, that something is clear—until the mistake costs him a friend or a job or an important sale.

A university president once learned this lesson the hard way. A shabby-looking couple asked him how much money it cost to run a university. Sizing them up as stupid yokels, he gave a curt answer. If only he had chatted a little, and taken time to make sure he understood why they asked, he might have doubled his university's endowment. Instead of donating $34 million as they had planned, Senator and Mrs. Leland Stanford went home to found their own university.

The impatient university president had responded to the Stanfords in terms of his own attitudes. This is a common cause of trouble. I heard of one company staff meeting at which the sales manager flew into a rage and shut off a factory supervisor who said, "We've got to stop making saws." Saws happened to be a sore point in the sales department. The manager never heard the full statement, which would have been, "We've got to stop making saws until Friday, because a shipment of steel is late."

Even when there's no misunderstanding people often surprise us. They react hotly to a seemingly harmless remark because we've blundered onto an invisible sore spot. Negotiators must be ready to adjust for such surprises.

For example, I once did a television interview with Charles F. Richter, the famous seismologist, shortly after one of California's larger earthquakes. He was a meek, gentle type so my interview seemed rather dull for a while. He evidently was preoccupied with weightier matters. He answered my questions mildly and almost absent-mindedly, until I asked if he had any idea where or when the next earthquake might occur.

The result was an emotional unheaval that must have measured about 8.6 on the Richter Scale. The professor leaped to his feet and shook a finger in my face. "God damn it, don't you dare ask me that question! If you want to ask about that, I'm leaving right now!"

When someone is angry, you must reassure him or you'll get nowhere. But you can't reassure him until you detect why he's angry. So I had to put myself instantly into Dr. Richter's shoes. He'd been studying earthquakes for forty-five years; he was the leading authority on them. Yet he couldn't answer the most important question about them, the question that people must have asked him incessantly. His inability to predict earthquakes was eating away at his pride.

So I hastened to say that I'd phrased my question inadequately, and that this interview was being taped, so that we could easily cut out my question and his response. This soothed him a bit; if it hadn't he certainly would have walked out that instant. I went on to explain, "What I meant to ask was whether any studies are being made, any tests or experiments that may some day give advance indications of earthquakes." "Oh yes," he said mildly, "many things were being done," and he went on to tell about them. The interview was saved.

BE SLOW TO JUDGE

A friend of mine who worked inside an office asked his sales manager for a chance at outside selling. The manager promised him the next opening. Soon it became known that an outside salesman planned to retire in a few months and that the sales manager was interviewing young job applicants. Then one day my friend saw the sales manager sit down with an applicant and the salesman who planned to retire. When he overheard the manager tell the applicant to go with the salesman on his rounds, my friend stalked out and resigned by mail.

It did look as if he'd been passed over. But his mistake was in acting on appearances as if they were established facts. He didn't know that two vacancies, not one, were opening up and that the first was to be his.

In another company, the manager of marketing mapped out a new route for a delivery truck driver. The driver said "But—."

The manager broke in, "I haven't time to argue. Follow that route."

The driver shrugged and drove off as instructed. He knew he would come to a low overpass that his trailer couldn't get under. When he did, he phoned and explained. The manager's refusal to listen in the first place cost his company a driver's wasted day, plus the anger of customers whose deliveries were delayed.

Such sad cases point out the lesson: Words and appearances are often deceptive. Don't jump to conclusions, especially when you're trying to win cooperation. But be ready to shift ground if the other fellow gets mad.

Right or wrong, your adversary feels more friendly when you encourage him to go into full detail about whatever is bothering him. By remembering this principle, I once managed to ease past a major difficulty with the government of Jordan.

I went to that country with my family and a camera crew to shoot a TV special to be called "Christmas in the Holy Land with the Linkletters." Another crew was in Israel, where I would join them later. But when I landed at the airport in Jordan a high-ranking Arab official met me. "We have decided to revoke your permission to take pictures," he told me.

I managed to keep calm. Instead of waving my contract in his face or demanding to see someone of even higher rank, I just asked mildly why the permit was revoked. He growled, "Because our intelligence people inform us that you have shipped twice as much raw film to Israel."

The Jordanians had jumped to the conclusion that I was biased in Israel's favor. How to convince them otherwise?

I didn't try to prove immediately that the quantity of film made little difference, although this was the key fact. An experienced persuader is often happy to appear ignorant and let the other guy show how smart he is. So I said, "Maybe I don't understand all the available opportunities for pictures. Do you have a map that shows each place having to do with Christ?"

Of course he had. He proudly showed me that there were as many, or more, historical sites on Jordan's side of the border.

I already knew this. But I made clear that I was deeply impressed. "May I show this map at the very beginning of my film?" I asked.

So now he was nodding his head instead of saying No. I went

on, "I guarantee that we'll do equal coverage. . . . The only reason I sent extra film into Israel is because we plan to shoot some interior scenes there—showing a Christmas party, re-enacting the ceremony where Jesus turned water into wine. Interior scenes use more film, of course." He not only okayed my plans, but gave so much help that it was embarrassing.

Looking back on the situation, I think what saved it was my early remark, "Maybe I don't understand." Isn't this worth saying, and sincerely thinking, when we run into opposition? Often we really don't understand. Maybe our opponent is right and we're wrong. But if he's the one who misunderstood, by listening we can learn the cause of the difficulty and probably can see how to clear it up.

By and large Americans are poor listeners. We talk more than we listen. Living in a competitive culture, we're chiefly concerned with expressing our own views and we tend to find other people's remarks a tedious interruption.

Moreover, what we lack in knowledge we sometimes try un-consciously to make up for by talking fast or loud and by gestur-ing emphatically. As Bertrand Russell pointed out, the heat of one's emotion varies inversely with one's knowledge of the facts. The less people know about a subject, the more they argue. And the less they listen. "You're not living up to the agreement. . . . We are too! . . . You're a liar! . . . You're another!" We hear it everywhere from kindergarten to the United Nations Security Council.

Even when people sit quietly and seem to absorb all the facts we feed them, their minds can be closed. Scores of people drown every year because they dive in too soon after eating; yet every-one has heard how dangerous this is. Millions ignore all the published warnings that cigarettes may cause cancer.

Driver education courses fail to cure teenagers of driving too fast, seeking thrills, and showing off. The National Advisory Council on Drug Abuse, to which I've devoted much time in recent years, has found that giving kids the frightful facts about drugs doesn't reduce the number who get hooked. Emotion, not education, is the biggest influence on action. People don't accept advice just because they know it's right.

We must work very hard to help them choose the right course of their own free will. The more they talk, the better our chance of influencing them. By listening, we can usually help them talk themselves around to a wise course of action. Or at least we can figure out what makes them tick, what to say to reach their emotions as well as their intellects. We should never say, or even think, "Shut up and listen to me!"

How about you? When someone challenges one of your cherished notions, do you say, "That's interesting. Tell me more," or do you instantly label him as not worth listening to? "Just another of those soft-headed educators," or "That's the old fundamentalist pitch," or "The guy is a fool." Do you wait alertly for a flaw in his arguments so you can pounce on it, meanwhile rehearsing what you'll say the next time you can grab the floor? Then you're not really listening. And you foreclose your chances of winning him to your way of thinking.

Learning to listen isn't hard, just unusual. It's an extremely important knack in salesmanship, in negotiation, in family life, and in every other enterprise where persuasion is needed.

THE KNACK OF LISTENING

Good listening demands active mental participation. It means trying to see the subject as the speaker sees it. To do this you think along with him, imagine yourself in his shoes, try to enter his private world, and understand how life looks to him.

As the first step in doing this, make a resolution: "I will refrain from mentally agreeing or disagreeing with anyone, refrain from praising or criticizing his views, until I'm sure what those views are."

As the second step, ask questions, either silently or aloud, while you listen.

Good listeners try to find something interesting in whatever is being said, something that can be put to use even if the talk is about a subject that seems dull. Is the speaker reporting anything new? Is he advocating a feasible idea? If unfeasible, could it be changed to improve it? What insight into his character can I get from what he's saying?

When the talk is about something that concerns you, there are many more questions to ask. You need to understand not only what the other fellow really thinks, but why he thinks it. When is he dealing in facts, when in inferences? If he purports to be stating facts, how does he know they're accurate? What is he leading up to? Has he left out something important? What are his needs and motives?

If you put your questions aloud, be careful not to give any impression that you're skeptical, hostile, derisive, or challenging. Any such negative response would simply stir up emotions and bring on mental deafness. Unfriendly questions elicit heat, not light.

Your questions must clearly be prompted by curiosity about the other fellow's views. Phrase them as requests for clarification: "Can you tell me more about . . . ?" "What are some of the pros and cons of this idea?" "Would you go into more detail on that point?" Probably the best question of all at this stage is something like, "Let's see if I can restate in my own words what I think you mean. Then will you tell me whether I've got it straight?"

This one simple precaution can prevent most friction and nearly all misunderstandings. It's a favorite tactic of my good friend Dave Mahoney, one of the fastest-rising executives became the new chairman of Norton Simon Incorporated. He says, "The only way I can prove to you that I really hear you is to repeat back what you're saying. Many times we find that areas of disagreement are narrowing as we get more precise."

When the parties to a dispute realize that they are being understood, that someone sees how the facts look to them, their statements get less exaggerated and less defensive. As Beardsley Ruml used to say, "Reasonable men always agree if they understand what they are talking about."

LISTEN FOR SMALL CLUES

As a third step in good listening, learn to listen between the lines. Someone talking may hide what he really feels or thinks. You can often sense this if you notice his tone of voice, his hesitations, his eyes, or his bodily movements. And if he keeps straying from the subject, you'll probably learn more by letting him ramble. Maybe he needs to get something off his chest.

Contrarily, if he talks guardedly you may open him up by encouraging him: "And what else? . . . What do you think that meant? . . . Can you explain in more detail?"

Either way, you're groping pleasantly for clues to how he thinks. Eisenhower had a friendly way of probing without putting a man on the defensive. "I can't get this through my thick head," he'd say. "Can you make it clearer?"

Applied in salesmanship, good listening is the low-pressure "customer-problem" approach to selling, as opposed to the old high-pressure fast-talking techniques. When Milo Perkins set out to sell burlap bags a half-century ago, the salesmen's textbooks said, "Brush up your arguments when you hit the road"; but he avoided arguments, and instead tried to find an area of agreement. He asked questions. Sometimes he would sit with a buyer and try to figure out the trend of the market—were bags going up or down? Sometimes he would even advise the customer not to buy until the market turned. His eye was on long-range mutual advantages, not on making a quick buck.

He was one of the first of what is now a widely successful type of salesman.

When you listen, your vocal agility becomes less important. How you talk becomes relatively unimportant because what you say, when it is guided by your listening, gives power to your words. To put this another way, your listening becomes an on-the-spot form of customer research that can immediately be put to work in improving your sales talk. In trying for any sale, the deeper insight you get into the prospect's problems, the greater your chance of selling him.

Beyond this, listening is a magnetic force that pulls people toward you. There is no surer way to make people like you than to pay them the compliment of interest and sympathy. Naturally they prefer to deal with someone who is interested in them.

A KIND OF HYPNOTISM

I suppose one key to my success as an interviewer in radio and TV has been sympathetic, encouraging, thoughtful listening. Some interviewers, instead of thinking about what their guest is saying, spend the time thinking up a wisecrack or another question. So their interviews go nowhere.

Most people being interviewed feel insecure, children most of all. Take a five-year-old and put him in front of lights and cameras and a big audience of strangers; what are the chances of getting him to say much? Almost nil. But I found that by looking him in the eye unwaveringly, never glancing around, never seeming amused or shocked, never demeaning his replies no matter how ridiculous, always staying on his level—by doing all this I virtually hypnotized him, narrowing his focus of attention to me exclusively so that he talked naturally. I realized that if I could do this with a child I could do it with adults. Try it.

On the other hand, when you don't listen to the other fellow, don't seem interested in him, he resents it and may hold it against you. I heard of a case in which an executive was arrested for slugging his boss outside the office, while under the influence of strong waters. When he was asked why he did it, he first pleaded intoxication. But finally he confessed that he had hated the other man for years. Why? Because, he said, "The manager walked through the office and never talked to anyone."

Likewise, when another company made an opinion survey and solicited anonymous comments from its employees, one man wrote, "Who does our department head think he is? The chief of police or something? He acts like it costs him money when we say anything to him."

These certainly weren't typical situations. But it is typical of human nature to resent aloofness or seeming aloofness. The way you listen has a crucial effect on the way people talk to you and think about you.

On higher levels of business, good listening is even more valuable. Searching questions by an outsider can turn up business opportunities that insiders may have overlooked because of their own closeness to the situation.

As a director of Royal Crown Cola, I racked my brain for ways to help the company increase sales. It was a poor third to Coca-Cola and Pepsi-Cola, both of which had far more money for advertising, more merchandising muscle, and more public acceptance. I asked Royal Crown's research and development people, "What's different about Royal Crown?" They gave me technical answers that I knew wouldn't interest the public.

But I kept probing, rather desperately. Eventually a researcher remarked, "Here's something that has nothing to do with Royal Crown, so it's probably not worth mentioning, but we do have another cola drink that we've been experimenting with. It contains no sugar, yet it doesn't have a bitter aftertaste. We've been thinking of calling it Diet-Rite."

He'd given us the answer to our problem. Royal Crown became the first low-calorie soft drink offered to the general public instead of just to diabetics. It led the whole new trend to sugarless sweeteners. Both Pepsi and Coke had to follow. The opportunity might have been locked away for years in a lab, if an outsider hadn't asked questions and listened to the answers.

In any organization, leaders and supervisors find at least three important reasons for listening to even the lowliest subordinate: (1) Only by listening can they spot coming trouble. (2) Nobody knows the problems of a job so well as the person doing it. (3) Employees want to feel their superiors are interested in them. When asked to describe a good manager, their most frequent answer is, "He takes an interest. You can talk to him "

5-- *LISTEN WHEN YOU TALK, TOO*

Feedback: A Key to Persuasiveness

As I emphasized in Chapter 4, few people are good listeners. When you're on the sending end, what can you do about this? How can you make sure that people hear and understand what you say?

You stay alert for feedback: for indications of the other person's reaction.

Let me begin with some sad examples of what happens when feedback is lacking. My own failure to listen as I talked almost cost me my whole career.

Lincoln Dellar, the manager of Station KGB in San Diego, gave me a part-time job as a radio announcer toward the end of my junior year at San Diego State. He needed a college student who could be trained for full-time announcing duties. He warned me, "Remember now, if you take this part-time job and make good, you'll obviously have to give up your senior year at college." After some thought, I agreed.

I worked all summer as an announcer and got along well. But as fall approached, I realized I had made a big mistake. My senior year would be the year I'd dreamed about since I was a freshman—the culmination of all my strivings. I was to be

63

captain of the basketball team, president of my fraternity, president of the Associated Men Students, production manager of the annual college show, active in debating, and so on. These activities meant so much to me that I couldn't bring myself to pass them up.

At last, feeling terribly guilty, I walked into Lincoln Dellar's office and poured out all the reasons why I must break my agreement with him. He kept nodding and saying he understood, he had gone to college too, everything would be okay. When I finally ran out of words I stood up, shook hands, and headed for the door. I had quit and he had accepted my resignation, I thought.

He called after me, "Linkletter, you haven't been listening at all, have you?"

It turned out he had been saying that he had realized my predicament and had figured out a way to keep me on part-time, so I could stay in college for my senior year. How lucky I was that he didn't get mad because I'd paid no attention to him while I talked! My subsequent work at KGB gave me my start in show business.

Another time, long afterward, I sent a memo explaining an animated drawing I needed for a TV commercial: "A picture of a stationary core with three or four small dots circling around." I followed up by asking the technician, "Do you get what I mean?" He nodded. No more was said. That was where both of us went wrong.

In the film I was dismayed to see the dots moving in separate circles, each in a corner of the screen. I had wanted them to circle like planets around the sun. I would have saved $1,000 and a lot of time if the technician had rephrased my order in different words: "You want each dot chasing its tail in a corner. Right?" Or I myself could have said to him, "I'm not sure I've made my idea clear. Just to see if we understand each other, can you put it in your own words?"

Count Helmuth von Moltke the elder, one of the great military organizers and commanders, told his generals before the Franco-Prussian War, "Remember, gentlemen, any instruction which can be misunderstood *will* be misunderstood." It's still true.

TAKE ENOUGH TIME

A foreman noticed a dangerous heap of oily waste around a machine. He told the machinist, "Better clean up around here." He wanted the man to put the waste in the trash can. But the machinist stopped production for an hour while he hunted up a janitor, borrowed a broom and dust pan, and gave the floor a thorough sweeping. Neither he nor the foreman had thought of checking to see whether he really understood. No feedback.

Take time to be sure you're getting your meaning across to everyone who needs to know. Being too brief can anger people as well as mislead them. Any important job of instruction or persuasion takes time.

U.S. Marine officers, famous for building morale and teamwork, are taught to use a powerful yet simple principle whenever they order men into action: "Tell 'em why!"

Telling why is also important when you must say no to someone. Show that you've given his request real thought. And be sure that you actually do give it thought. It's the peremptory brush-off that causes resentment. Clarence Lyons, a well-known and well-liked banker in New York, used to say, "You must make the person see that you understand his problem, especially when you have to say No."

I've known several insurance adjusters who approved millions of dollars in payments each year, yet often had to say No. However, they always took plenty of time to show sympathy for the claimant. They would explain that morally they might agree with him, but in this case the company's attorneys had ruled that the insured had no liability. "So you see my hands are tied," one of them would say sadly. "I have no power to make a voluntary payment which the law doesn't require."

Vance Packard tells about a neighbor of his, an interior decorator, who never says No to clients when they want to put some discordant decoration into their homes. Instead the decorator gently educates them to say Yes to what he wants them to do. For example, one couple built a modern home with floor-to-ceiling windows and open layout. The wife wanted flowery chintz curtains, definitely wrong for that house. The decorator said, "Let's go through the house and see what you want your curtains to do."

As they walked, he got her talking about the functions the curtains would serve in each room and what fabrics would harmonize best with the modern decor. After a while the lady forgot her passion for chintz.

In any family and in any organization people hate to be told what to do if they don't understand why. Blind obedience isn't part of the American character.

Our space exploration program was slowed because of this. Delicate microminiaturized electronic parts kept malfunctioning. Finally the trouble was traced to assembly lines where women were under orders to discard their rubber gloves and put on a fresh pair after handling each part. They didn't because it seemed wasteful to them, until an executive finally explained that invisible film on gloves could ruin the apparatus.

I've heard innumerable tales of messages which backfired because they were too brief. An office manager shifted his best tabulating machine operator from a complex machine to a simpler model. She quit. To the manager the move had been a stopgap to meet temporary needs. But he hadn't told her so. She saw it as a humiliating demotion.

A group of draftsmen stopped work because air conditioners were installed in their department. Their boss was mystified; he had thought he enhanced their comfort. Eventually he learned they were angry just because he hadn't asked—nor even told— them about the change. So he spent hours explaining how the air conditioners were chosen, by whom, and why, and why there wasn't time to discuss it first with the draftsmen. Their self-respect restored, they resumed work.

Using this principle can save grief at home as well as at work. Whenever we make a decision we can ask ourselves, "Who needs to know about this? Who might be perturbed if he doesn't understand my reason?" If you want to be persuasive, don't be the strong silent type. As Sir Francis Bacon pointed out, "Silence is the virtue of fools."

WATCH YOUR LANGUAGE

Avoid words that may puzzle your listener, or may have several meanings. Telephone company men learn not to use jargon like "work a divided trick" with new operators. Even a simple phrase can have many meanings, as author Barrows Dunham proves with "pretty little girls' camp." Is the camp pretty? Is it little? Or neither? Dunham says, "If there can be so much obscurity in language apparently simple, how much more will there be in statements with complex syntax and an abundance of formidable words?"

Many specialists can't express themselves well enough to be understood outside their specialty, so they fail at teamwork and persuasion (except maybe with colleagues). But wiser men expect to be misunderstood; they take pains to help the other fellow grasp their thought. As they talk or write, they challenge themselves: "Can this possibly be misunderstood? Can I make it plainer, or more pleasant?"

WHAT FEEDBACK CAN DO

The biggest mistake made by publicists, teachers, and statesmen is to think that if they simply point out the right course,
everyone will follow it. As we saw in Chapter 4, the fullest,
clearest explanation won't necessarily change people's minds.
But simple give-and-take conversation can gradually do the job
where one-way exhortation fails.

For example, a government nutrition expert in Iowa undertook a campaign to persuade housewives to use more milk. He
gave them solid, factual, easy-to-understand lectures. He also
was smart enough to get feedback, by checking to see how many
of his listeners actually began using more milk. He found that
only 16 percent did so. Then he became smarter yet. Instead of
lecturing, he contrived for small undirected discussion groups to
talk over the question, "Should we use more, or less, milk?" Its
use jumped 50 percent.

Do you talk too much? Beware of enchantment with the
sound of your golden voice. Beware of concentrating solely on
yourself and what you're saying. Concentrate instead, with part
of your mind, on the spoken and unspoken signals from whoever
you're trying to persuade or enlighten.

If you're alert, you can detect the small signs that people are
tuning you out. When it does happen, you need to find out why,
then figure out how to overcome their mental deafness. Otherwise you're wasting your words. You can't communicate with
puzzled or hostile people until you get in step with them.

Dostoevski made a profound remark in *The Brothers
Karamazov:* "If people around you are spiteful and callous and
will not hear you, fall down before them and beg their for-
giveness; for in truth you are to blame for their not wanting
to hear you." Most adverse situations are, at least in part,
created by ourselves.

I remember a sales manager whose men tuned out for

completely mysterious reasons when he made one simple request of them. He asked them to compute certain figures on the basis of their own sales. The job was easy, but the silent resistance to doing it was stiff. So the manager, instead of pounding the desk or threatening, kept drawing his men into casual chats which gradually got around to the computations they weren't making. Finally he got enough feedback to discover the trouble.

Three years earlier, a bossy and villainous sales manager had tried to get the same computations. So this simple matter was a symbol of Simon Legree to the salesmen. Their reaction was emotional. Once he had solved the mystery, the sales manager temporarily dropped his request and waited for his men to develop more familiarity with him. Then he asked again and easily got what he asked.

How can you tell when such symbols may be turning off your listeners? Mainly by knowing about the people you're talking to—their past history, their prejudices and allegiances. For example, if your listeners are staunch union men, you needn't be surprised if they turn stony-faced when you praise the National Association of Manufacturers. Whenever you run into unexpected, extraordinary coldness to a proposal, it's a tip-off to look for some symbolic meaning.

More commonly, however, the trouble may be merely that you're pressing too hard, talking too much. Eugene C. Peckham's pamphlet, *Dynahelps for Democratic Leaders* gives some good prescriptions for negotiators who realize they talk too much and want to cut down. One is to put their thoughts in writing before they speak. This makes them clarify and condense. Another is to ask a question instead of stating an opinion. A third is simply to lower the voice. "The chances are you have a strident voice," Peckham says, "or you wouldn't so successfully overwhelm others who want to talk. Turn down your volume."

The talkative are chronic interrupters. "Practice yielding," Peckham suggests. "When someone tries to interrupt you, let

him. When a silence falls, wait for someone else to break it."
If you can do that, you've kicked the habit.

IS ANYONE LISTENING?

Good teachers keep asking questions to see if pupils understand and to keep them thinking. Good salesmen do, too.
Putting your thought in question form, instead of stating it
bluntly, can open up deaf ears. People who get along with
others seldom begin, "My advice to you is ... " or, "The fact
is. ... " Instead they ask, "Do you think it would help if ... "
or, "What would happen if we ... " or, "Shall we talk about
your ... ?"

Costly mistakes caused by poor listening have made many
executives afraid of oral communication. Nevertheless, "Put it
in writing" is the wrong rule for most situations. It's easier to
misread a written message than a spoken one.

The man who writes a memo or a letter loses all chance to
make his message better understood through his tone of voice,
facial expression, gestures, his whole manner. Worse yet, memos
and letters may be only half-read or buried in heaps of other
paper. A written communicator isn't likely to get any feedback
at all. He may never know whether or not his words were read,
understood, believed, or acted on.

Feedback comes easily in the give-and-take of talk. One very
successful personnel expert told me, "We'd rather work belly-to-
belly than throw memos over the fence."

Still, there are times when you have no choice but to communicate in writing. Then seeking feedback becomes more important than ever. Make it as easy as possible for recipients of
any written message to let you know how they feel about it.

This is standard policy nowadays in many well-run companies. They want feedback from employees in order to improve management. Today, about one company in four takes

polls to get facts that don't flow upward easily—such as whether employees are really listening to what management tells them.

For example, at Burlington Northern Railroad, any employee can blow off steam through a new "dial BOSS" program. A telephone recorder takes his message. He is guaranteed written replies from bosses. He is also guaranteed that his immediate superiors won't be told his identity. I hear that the program is working wonders for morale, and has generated lots of good suggestions that might otherwise not have been offered—or listened to.

MEETING OPPOSITION

When met by noncommittal silence, good persuaders know that it probably signals some degree of resistance—maybe puzzlement, maybe skepticism, maybe downright disbelief or dislike. So they try hard to coax this negative feeling out into the open where they can deal with it. They ask questions.

If possible they ask questions that are likely to bring a Yes. Psychologically, saying Yes a few times can soften a person's negative feelings. It shows him that there's some agreement between him and his supposed adversary. So he feels more receptive, if only subconsciously.

Yet even if he says No he's given more help than if he keeps his mouth shut. There's a familiar saying among salesmen, "The sale begins when the customer says No." Until the customer opens his mouth you have few clues to what he's thinking.

Even if he's totally wrong and stubborn, you avoid arguing with him. An argument is a clash of egos. If you win, you wound the other man's ego. "A man convinced against his will is of the same opinion still," as the old jingle goes.

Long ago the Penn Mutual Life Insurance Company gave its salesmen strict orders: "Don't argue." Other sales organizations now follow similar policies. Crown Zellerbach salesmen are instructed not to take No for an answer unless they've been turned down five times, yet they never try to beat down a No by a frontal attack. Wise old Ben Franklin used to say, "If you argue and rankle and contradict, you may achieve a victory sometimes. But it will be an empty victory, because you will never get your opponent's good will."

Patrick J. O'Haire, a red-haired, hot-tempered Irishman, became a star salesman for the White Motor Company when he learned how to handle turndowns. Here, in his own words, is his way of meeting objections:

"When I walk into a buyer's office and he says: 'What? A White truck? They're no good! I wouldn't take one if you gave it to me. I'm gonna buy the Whoozis Truck,' then I say: 'Brother, the Whoozis is a good truck. You'll never make a mistake buying it. The Whoozis is made by a fine company and sold by good people.'

"He's speechless then. There's no room for an argument. He can't keep on saying 'It's the best,' when I'm agreeing with him. We then get off the subject of Whoozis and I begin to talk about the good points of the White truck."

PERSUASION IS PROBLEM-SOLVING

When you set out to persuade an opponent, your real mission is to help him think through a problem.

His objections and questions are part of his thinking. By showing you understand, you can then get him listening to your side. Let's suppose you run into the most common of all objections, "It costs too much. I can get something comparable at a lower price." Here's one way you might think along with him:

"You're right. I'm glad you brought that up. In these days it's important to buy economically, isn't it? Of course the purchase price is just part of your total cost, right? Now what about the other costs of whatever you buy? Shall we talk about costs of repair, replacement, turnover, wear and tear?"

Get a pencil in his hand and get him making his own calculations of these other items. If he is a retailer, he ties up money in inventory if a product on his shelves doesn't move fast. If he is a manufacturer, when a part of one of his machines has to be replaced often, he is laying out money every time he buys a new one. If he is in a service business, when he buys a tool that does an inferior job, then he is risking damage to whatever he uses it on, and the costs of repairing the damage may add up to more than he saves by buying cheaply. And so on.

When you've got him agreeing, then you can say, "Now let's see if my product can save you money, even though it's higher priced. Here are some figures. . . ."

Don't blame him if he keeps on objecting. Maybe he's right.

Ask yourself: Where have I failed? Am I listening enough? Do I really dig his objections? Are they valid? If they are, why should I try to talk him into doing something against his best interests? A dishonest persuader has a hard time living with himself.

LEAVE ROOM TO SHIFT

Avoidance of showdowns is part of the honest strategy of letting someone see it your way. Saving face is vital. No one likes to give in.

And the mature negotiator cares more about being understood than about proving others wrong. So when he is met by disagreement, he listens carefully and often finds that his critic has misunderstood. In that case he first says, "I see your point. In other words—," and restates the criticism even more vividly and convincingly if possible.

Then he goes on, "I didn't make my own point clear. I stated it badly. Let's see if I can explain it better." This lets the listener off the hook, coaxes him to listen, and allows him to change his position without admitting he was wrong.

It's just as important to avoid putting yourself on a limb with a dogmatic statement from which you can't shift gracefully. Most issues are not black or white. Your point of view is not the only one. There may be arguments you haven't thought of or facts you don't know. Whether as a parent, salesman, or boss, you'll get better understanding if you encourage feedback by beginning, "Doesn't it seem to you that . . . " or "Can you tell me whether . . . ?"

Historians say that Britain's outmanned air force beat the Luftwaffe because British air marshals stood up to Churchill while their Nazi counterparts didn't dare argue with Goering. Probably this means that Churchill was alert to feedback. Or it could mean that Churchill's staff was more tactful and persuasive than the Germans. Maybe they studied his reactions and learned how not to arouse his famous stubbornness with any imputation that he was wrong.

One young American aide learned how to offer criticism to generals and get away with it. He always began by showing respect: "Sir, will the general permit a question?" And then he phrased his criticism in the form of a question that ruffled no feathers: "Would the position be better if . . . ?"

Even when you get unavoidably embroiled in a hot argument, it's a good idea to show that you're thinking along with the other person, no matter how unreasonable he may be: "I'd be angry, too if my window were broken." "If I were in your position I'd probably do just what you've done." When the other fellow knows that you've really listened, really understood him, he can't help feeling friendlier. And he can compromise without losing face.

You can cool down the situation further with more subtle semantic devices. Instead of stating a fact bluntly, you can ease into it with the phrase, "As far as I know—" And when you want to express disagreement, you can meet your opponent halfway by beginning, "Up to a point, you're probably right in saying—" and then, after repeating his statement in his own words, you can show where you think it goes wrong.

This same tactic works well in reverse. When you want to express an opinion (if you must resort to one, instead of sticking to facts) you can phrase it as a question: "Up to what point would I be right in saying . . . ?"

THE GOLDEN RULE

"Who are the best communicators in business?" *Nation's Business* once asked, and answered itself:

"Those who communicate best are those who understand that communication starts with what the other guy needs. They concern themselves not only with the idea of getting their own ideas across but whether the listener is equal to what they want to say. They are also concerned about getting feedback whether it is written, verbal, or even a mass meeting. Communication is function of exchange. And communication is effective in direct proportion to participation."

Norio Ochi, chief executive director of the spectacularly successful Japan Trade Center of New York, says that Japanese rate this principle highest of all in marketing: "We insist upon getting to know the other person's point of view because to us it is the key to successful communications."

When you're a good listener, both you and the other fellow go away from even a quick exchange of words with a warm feeling inside. There has been communication. The very word "communicate" comes from roots meaning "to make common." Its purpose is to turn an idea into a shared possession.

Reaching others is not a trick. It is the legitimate business of finding what we have in common. It boils down to two simple questions: Do I make myself clear? Do I understand? The common denominator is consideration for other people which, after all, is just our ancient golden rule.

6 -- *PATIENCE OR PUSH?*

When to Go Slow, When Fast

"We might be interested some day," the president of Alcoa murmured politely. "If you have something good in mind, let me hear from you."

"Don't say it if you don't mean it," replied my friend Bill Zeckendorf, the salesman and entrepreneur who had put together the world's largest real estate empire. "I don't want to waste your time or mine."

Frank Magee, the silver-haired president of Alcoa, looked slightly startled at this stern warning. "Well, I can't commit myself. But I'd be glad to hear from you."

Zeckendorf casually dismissed the subject: "Oh, I've nothing in mind right at the moment. But if something should come up, I'll call you."

To say he had nothing in mind was less than candid. He hoped that somebody would pay $43 million for 260 acres of movie studio land in the heart of Los Angeles, land on which he had proposed to build a big complex of office buildings, apartment towers, theaters, restaurants, and shops to be called Century City. Zeckendorf's dreams had outrun his resources and he was on the brink of bankruptcy.

77

But this wasn't the time to broach such an immense deal to Alcoa's chief executive, whom he barely knew. The two men merely happened to be seated together at a business executives' luncheon in Manhattan. Zeckendorf, as always, had taken the first chance to turn the talk to the topic of real estate and had twitted Magee on Alcoa's apparent lack of interest in it. Urban development might be a profitable long-term investment for the aluminum company. But when the lunch broke up, Zeckendorf was not sure whether he had any chance of getting Alcoa interested.

In the next four months he tried everywhere else he could think of to find someone with the vision and the financial muscle to undertake the Century City project. In mid-August 1960, with few prospects left in view and no money to pay a debt of $2.5 million which was due, he determined to make the most of the faint encouragement Frank Magee had given him. He picked up the phone and called Pittsburgh. "Frank, remember that chat we had some time ago?"

Magee allowed that he did.

"Well, I've got something."

Magee murmured, "Fine. Let me know some time when you'd like to come down."

Zeckendorf preferred to stalk big game slowly, but time was running out for him. He said, "I'm letting you know now."

"When do you want to come?" Magee asked politely.

"Tomorrow."

Magee coughed and mumbled something about short notice.

"I asked if you were serious last time, so this is not short notice," Zeckendorf said. "If you're busy, I'll come the next day." Then, to soften the abrupt demand, he added, "The reason I want to come tomorrow is that I have a date at Westinghouse, and I can come over and see you before lunch."

Magee agreed to see him at 10:30. Zeckendorf arrived punctually for the most critical negotiation of his long career. Most of Alcoa's top executives were assembled. Zeckendorf had never met any of them. Magee made the introductions, sat back and said, "Well, tell us the story."

In his own office Zeckendorf was a notable showman. He sometimes confided to his staff that "our office lends credence to our ideas." He loved to manipulate dials at his desk, adjusting the colors and brightness of various lights for "mood control" while he talked. He used color slides, movies, flip charts, sample panels of structural materials, and a pageant of eloquent expert witnesses. He sometimes spent as much as $200,000 on miniature buildings to help prospective backers visualize the wondrous developments he had in mind. (In Chapter 2 we saw Kaiser and other great salesmen using this technique.) But there was no setting, no chance for exhibits in Pittsburgh. Zeckendorf's persuasion kit contained only a map of the site.

JUST THE FACTS

This turned out to be all for the best. The Alcoa men were conservatives who would have resisted a spectacular presentation. So he talked quietly about what might be done with the open land in Los Angeles. The group listened impassively.

Now came the crucial moment. He had to tell them the staggering price. But he had thought of a legitimate way to make it look more attractive.

"The price," he said, "is forty-three million. But it need cost you only eighteen million."

They waited skeptically.

He explained that the movie studio expected to lease back eighty acres for its own use. "That lease can be sold for twenty-five million," he went on. "So if you want to sell that off, your exposure is only eighteen million. With that amount you'll be buying the best of the land. . . . Of course you'll spend another eight or ten million developing the land with roads, utilities, sewers, bridges, landscaping and other things. For this expense you'll have six million square feet fully developed for use, at a cost of roughly four dollars a square foot. In time that land could easily be worth fifty dollars a square foot."

Magee asked what role Webb & Knapp, Zeckendorf's company, would play in the transaction. Zeckendorf said, "You put up two-thirds of the money, and we'll put up the rest. We'll develop the property. We'll take two-thirds of the profit, you take one-third. But we all get our money back before profits are divided."

Someone raised a delicate question about the financial health of Webb & Knapp. Zeckendorf argued boldly that the huge debts were a testimony to his strength, not weakness. "A borrower must put up gold-plated collateral to get cash from those big lenders. They lend only on a sure thing, and then only less than they feel they can recover by immediate sale of the collateral. Only a very solid company could borrow as much as Webb & Knapp has."

After some further discussion, Magee asked Zeckendorf, "When do you want an answer on all this?"

"Today."

THE RUSH ACT

Around the room, mouths fell open. "How can we give an answer today?" Magee said. "This is so big, it's revolutionary. Look, Bill, you're talking about a bigger urban development than anything that private capital has ever undertaken in this country."

Zeckendorf stood up. "Well, Frank, if you won't give me an answer today, I'll have to go somewhere else. I told you before that you shouldn't ask me down unless you really meant to do business. That didn't mean you were committed to buy, but I thought you wanted to give it serious consideration, which means immediate consideration."

Bill Zeckendorf

No one spoke.

More calmly, to hide his tension, Zeckendorf suggested, "Why don't you fellows think it over? I'm going to have lunch at Westinghouse, and I can be free this afternoon after lunch. I'll come back."

After a long pause, Magee said, "All right, if that's convenient."

Zeckendorf left, wondering if he had pushed too hard. After all, nobody at Alcoa had even seen the land he was asking them to buy. And there was no time for them to check his cost estimates, or to verify that the movie company would really sell on the terms he suggested. If Zeckendorf had permitted it, Alcoa might have studied the matter for months. But he couldn't afford to permit any postponement. Lazard Freres, the investment bankers, could throw him into bankruptcy within the next few days if he did not produce their $2.5 million.

After lunch, the same group of men awaited him silently, their faces as expressionless as before. Magee began to talk in a monotone. Zeckendorf gathered he was explaining why Alcoa would not venture into real estate.

" . . . and we don't understand real estate," Magee concluded. "Nevertheless, we are going to do this."

He resumed talking in the same monotone. Zeckendorf told me later, "I heard what Magee said but I didn't grasp it for several seconds, and then I wondered if I'd heard right in the first place."

Finally Magee said, "Now, what do you want us to do?"

"Give me a deposit of two and a half million," Zeckendorf said at once.

Magee called across the room to the corporate treasurer, "Matt, you got two and a half million anywhere? All right, give Bill a check. What are you waiting for?"

That was how the great Century City development, which you must have seen if you've been in Los Angeles in the last decade, got started. For all their inscrutability, the Alcoa executives had been more receptive than Zeckendorf knew. They had been secretly convinced for some time that Alcoa ought to lend a hand with the rebuilding of American cities—partly because this could be profitable, partly because it would please the public, and partly because it would give Alcoa a chance to sell more aluminum to construction companies.

Alcoa had been wondering where to find a partner who knew the real estate business. It knew Zeckendorf well by reputation. And he had happened along at the right time with the right piece of land.

The story of this huge, quick deal illustrates an important principle: There are times—more times than most persuaders realize—when it pays to push for a quick decision.

"SOMEONE ELSE WANTS THIS"

I used this same principle, maybe by accident, when General Electric was interested in signing me to do a daily coast-to-coast show on CBS.

Like most corporations, GE wanted plenty of time to think it over. I wasn't in a position to allow this. I was already broadcasting a similar show called "What's Doing, Ladies?" for Safeway on the Pacific Coast, under a contract which was about to expire. So I had to tell GE, "Look, renewal time with Safeway is at hand. They're very happy with the show, and are ready to sign again. You'll have to put off any deal with me for a whole year unless you come to a decision within the next ten days."

(It helps in selling if you can say in effect, "Someone else is eager to buy this. But I want you to have a chance, if you can make up your mind quickly.")

"Why, Art, our lawyers couldn't even draw up a contract for you in ten days," the GE men protested.

"I realize that," I countered. "But on the basis of my belief in you, and our general agreement, I'm willing to go without a contract."

That did it. They put me on the air.

Here's an interesting footnote. GE's lawyers made the contract negotiations even more convoluted than usual. We still didn't have a contract when my GE show finally went off the air five years later.

WATCH FOR CHANCES TO CLOSE

When your proposition runs into no big objections, when your listeners seem to be seriously considering it even though they remain poker-faced, this is your cue to be aggressive. Suggest a quick agreement and see what happens. They will probably prefer to stall. But you mustn't mistake an excuse for an objection. Do your darnedest to impel them to act now.

Countless sales are lost, countless deals fall through, countless committees reach no decision merely because of postponement. A would-be persuader must watch and listen for his chance to get the signature on the contract or the final handshake or the vote for specific action.

As soon as the tide of any interview turns favorable, reject all doubt as Zeckendorf did and ride it to decision. The chance may not come again.

Once I watched Johnny Weissmuller, the famous old-time swimmer, teamed with a veteran carnival pitchman named Red Willever in an effort to sell $579 massage chairs at a home show. The plan was for Johnny to attract visitors into the booth by his presence, while Red handled the actual selling. Trying to sell one couple a chair, Red brought them to that critical moment when a customer teeters tantalizingly on the verge of a decision to buy. Crouched between the two massage chairs in which they were lolling, Red produced his order book, then made an inspired move to nudge them over the brink.

"Ask Johnny what he thinks," he urged the couple. "Go ahead."

Signing autographs a few feet away, Johnny caught his cue. He didn't make the blunder of launching into a long sales talk. He just gave the young fellow a shy glance. "Man, you won't regret it," he said softly.

The couple decided then and there to buy. What's more, they wanted to pay cash. Too bad the deal wasn't closed on the spot. Since they didn't have the necessary $500-plus on them, they said they would go home for the money and return next day, which they never did.

Many people are indecisive. They thrive on discussions and study groups and "going home to think about it." They may like something, they may secretly want it, they may be almost ready to accept it fully—but their minds are automatically groping for new exits so they won't have to sign the contract or fork over the money. Unless pushed, they don't act.

This is why the expert salesman is forever maneuvering for a possible close. He listens for feedback as he talks. At any stage his idea may click and the prospect will be ready to accept his proposition.

Early in the negotiations, he unobtrusively pulls out his order blank and puts it in plain sight. This avoids the awkward pause which would come if he stopped and fumbled for the papers at the psychological moment. And it gets the customer used to looking at it; he won't be frightened by it when the time comes to sign.

The salesman doesn't wait until the very end of his presentation to give the prospect a chance to say Yes. He provides many chances, what some salesmen call "trial closes" or "closing feelers."

He may pause and say, "Doesn't that make sense to you?" or, "Don't you agree?" or, "Is this the model you prefer?"

GENTLE PUSHING

As soon as the prospect has agreed to the main points of the proposal, the salesman shifts gears and acts as if full agreement has been reached. He begins to refer to the order blank, pointing out what it provides, and writing in the necessary data. He gently conveys the impression that both he and the customer are cooperating in making it accurate.

If the prospect hasn't really signified desire, a salesman may try for the close with "either-or" questions. He asks, "Which color do you like best? . . . Will you charge this, or would you rather pay cash? . . . Shall I send this to your house or to your office? . . . Can you spare the time to go over for the doctor's examination this afternoon? . . . Shall I put RUSH on this order?"

When the prospect is ready to sign, the tactful persuader avoids saying "Sign here." Those words are scary. Instead he says something like, "Be sure to write your name just as it appears above" or, "I'll go over the order again while you write your check" or, "Now if you give me your money I'll put this through immediately."

Similarly, in conferences or group negotiations a good leader senses when he can summarize and call for action. As a playwright does, he steers the dialogue toward a planned climax. Taking care not to sound bossy, he may say, "Let's see where we've got to. . . . Could we summarize the discussion so far something like this? . . . Are we agreed on these main points?"

WHEN TO STOP SELLING

Some men are direct and decisive. They soon grow impatient to get the talking finished. The likeliest way to reach a closing with them is to come frankly to the point, as Zeckendorf did. Overselling can spoil a sale. It takes alertness to see when we are saying too little or too much.

Konrad Bercovici, a famous author, used to tell how he wandered into an art gallery, took a fancy to a painting, and asked a clerk the price. If she had set a high figure he would have paid it, perhaps after a little bargaining. But she said the manager had just hung the painting. She wasn't sure of its price. So could he return the next day to discuss it with the manager? Her reluctance to sell only whetted Konrad's desire.

"I hardly slept that night," he recalled. "I knew I had discovered a work of art that I wanted. I was sure this unknown painter would soon be acclaimed as a master. I hurried back the next morning, fearing that someone else might buy the painting before I saw the manager."

But the manager pounced on him, praising the picture and flattering Konrad. "You have an appreciative eye. It is one of the finest works that has ever hung on these walls. This work will go down in history as a masterpiece, to be mentioned with Rembrandt and Raphael."

The more the manager talked, the more skeptical Konrad felt. He had just wanted to know the price. The only question was whether he could afford it. But now he wondered why this work of art needed such fulsome praise if it were really great. Had he overestimated it?

"I looked again," the writer said. "The painting was nice, but not in the class of masterworks he mentioned. As I waited through his long sales pitch, I saw flaws in the picture. My suspicion grew that he wanted to palm off an inferior painting on me. When the price was finally mentioned, I said I would think it over, and walked out."

There is a sequel. Years later this author saw the same painting in a friend's home. "As I stared, all my original love for the work returned. Meanwhile the artist had acquired a good reputation. If only the fool salesman hadn't tried to overwhelm me with his sales talk, that valuable and beautiful picture would be hanging on my wall."

You may have planned a strong sales talk, but you shouldn't necessarily make the prospect listen to the end. At any point where he accepts your proposition, stop. Don't bring up anything new.

UNSELLING A MAHARAJAH

Cartier's, the awesome store that sells millions of dollars worth of jewelry each year, once lost an important customer because a young salesman added an extra selling point after the customer said Yes. The salesman, Jules Glaenzer, never forgot the lesson he learned that day and eventually rose to be first vice-president of the company.

The Paris branch of Cartier's sent him to a maharajah who wanted a sapphire ring for his turban. Glaenzer had such a ring, a 150-carat stone worth $40,000. He showed it to the potentate and his appraiser, and waited while they conferred in Hindi. The appraiser told Glaenzer that His Highness would buy the ring.

Glaenzer started to quote the price, but the other man interrupted. Price was not to be mentioned, he said. The ruler would take the ring.

Glaenzer nodded happily. "As a matter of interest," he remarked as he rose to go, "His Highness might like to know that this ring was worn by Louis XVI of France."

When this was translated, the maharajah thought a moment, then made a curt remark to his companion, who announced, "The order is cancelled."

Why? Because His Highness didn't want his head chopped off, Glaenzer was told. Moral: We never know what superstitions or irrational feelings may kill a sale at the last minute.

QUICK SALES TO STRANGERS

Do you know there are salesmen today who, every ninety minutes from mid-morning to midnight, sell $500 worth of sewing machines, stereo sets, and assorted other goods? They do it without advertising, without huge signs or show windows. And they sell to people whose attention must be caught in mid-stride, while strolling along a boardwalk or a carnival midway.

These are the legendary pitchmen. I sometimes think that all salesmen and persuaders can learn something from them. If a pitchman's techniques can make strangers crowd around to thrust money into his hands, might not similar techniques be even more effective on behalf of a really worthwhile proposition? Maybe the carnival men know more about influencing human nature than most of us do.

The pitchman capitalizes on impulses. He makes people feel an impulse to grab a bargain (as Zeckendorf did with Alcoa). And he takes their money quickly, before they change their minds.

If you believe the carny barker is a dying breed, you're not exactly right. He may be around for a long time yet. Carnivals are more popular than ever. *Amusement Business,* the weekly paper of the carnival and circus industries, says that 113 million people a year visit the state and county fairs where most carnivals play. At least 500 tent and wagon shows crisscross the country during the March-through-October season. Some of them represent a capital investment of more than $500,000. And some of their pitchmen must be even more expert than the fabled old-timers, because today's public is more sophisticated and local police watch the midways to make sure there is no fraud. Despite the stiffer sales resistance, a number of carny salesmen earn well over $20,000 a year.

Chuck Bedell, one of the master pitchmen, was a good

friend of mine for years. I got acquainted with him in 1935, on the midway at the San Diego International Exposition, and later at the Texas Centennial Exposition in Dallas and the world's fairs in San Francisco and New York.

Sometimes Chuck sold gadgets. Sometimes big-ticket merchandise. Sometimes he coaxed people to try their hand at a "skill game." If he were running a ball-and-marble board, or some other variation of a game that in one form or another has entranced fairgoers since ancient times, he might stop a passing couple by asking, "How long you two been married, a month? . . . I got a wedding present for you—a free game!" Or he would attract a single stroller by shouting, "Hey buddy, you dropped something." The man would glance around the ground behind him. "Here it is," Chuck would bark, waving a card with FREE GAME printed on it.

"You get your free game right here," he continued. "Roll these marbles in the holes on this board. If you get the right score, you can take home any prize in this booth. Absolutely no charge."

The prizes included TV sets and radios. People are always lured by something for nothing. That's why so many package-goods companies attract new consumers by giving away free samples or "reduced-price" coupons; why mail-order firms offer "no-risk free trials." They learned from the carny people.

Hooked, Chuck's "mark" would accept the free game. To win, he had to get 100 points. He could play as long as it took to reach that total. But when the number 29 came up—as it often did, because of the percentages—he must pay fifty cents for the next roll.

MAKE IT EASY

To keep the player going beyond the first free game, Chuck fast-counts him into a 50-point score on his free roll: "Oh boy—

that's 5, 9, 16, 20, 28, 33, 44, you've got 50 points to start," Chuck says, swiftly scooping up the marbles. The next roll, costing fifty cents, usually brings a fast-count 20-pointer: "Gee, you got 70 points in just two rolls that means you only need 30 more to win!" The third or fourth roll, also for a half-dollar, very likely comes up 29. This ups the bet to a dollar. From there on, the pitchman takes what the traffic will bear—sometimes a hundred dollars or more.

When a mark has lost enough, Chuck must get him to swallow his losses philosophically, so there'll be no compaints to the police. To do this he begins what he calls the cool-out.

"Gee, you're having some bad luck," he says when the man has rolled several rounds without reaching 100. "People get into bad streaks sometimes. That's how this game is," he adds sympathetically after a few more losing rounds.

Finally Chuck calls a halt. "You're having a tough time. I'll give you two more rounds free, and if you lose we'll call it quits. Fair enough?" (Labor negotiators, UN diplomats, and other high-level persuaders often use similar cool-out strategy when negotiating from a position of strength. They offer minor concessions to sugarcoat defeat on the major issue.)

The mark always agrees that Chuck's offer is fair. Chuck then counts him into a 37, which carries the notation "HP" on the card of winning numbers. "That means 'house pays.' You get a prize," says Chuck, handing the man a large stuffed doll that costs a few dimes. "You get something after all." The player, poorer but not indignant, departs.

SELLING GADGETS

In the Depression, as I well remember, stockbrokers were making twelve dollars a week selling apples while pitchmen made fifty dollars peddling kitchen tools. Today there are still at least a hundred supersalesmen who specialize in what are known as bastard items, things that have to be demonstrated to be sold. The rubber mop, the electric scissors, the kitchen knife, the food grater, the juice extractor, the vegetable garnisher would only gather dust on the supermarket shelf. But put them in the hands of pitchmen and people elbow their way through the crowd to buy.

If you've been to the Los Angeles County Fair, to the Home Show in Boston, the Flower Show in Washington, or the Miss America Pageant in Atlantic City, you've seen these friendly spielers pouring hundreds of words per minute into a you-can't-live-without-it sales pitch. Combining old medicine-show razzle-dazzle with modern findings on mob psychology, they flourish from spring through Pageant Week, earning enough to winter in Florida.

TV celebrity Ed McMahon sold on Atlantic City's boardwalk for five years in the 1950s; actor Charles Bronson is another alumnus. Dave Clark, who started pitching foot medicine and vitamins during the Depression and later became famous on TV as the pitchman for Charles Antell hair formula, is still going strong at big county fairs, spending $500 a week for vegetables and fruit that he slices, trims, decorates, peels, squeezes, and carves during his hourly demonstrations.

"Years ago we had a lot of fakers in the business," Dave says. "But now ninety percent of the merchandise is legitimate. I work the same fairs year after year, and you can't do that if your merchandise is phony. Our goods are cheap because we sell in such volume."

How do these salesmen move gadgets? Roger Gilmore, who pitches a plastic juice extractor first sold at the 1938 World's Fair, says: "The secret is to sell yourself, to make yourself believable. You can see the people strolling past your booth and thinking, 'That guy isn't gonna sell me anything.' So you start gradually breaking them down, getting them interested. You pull them in as close as you can, by doing things that catch their eye and by jokes that amuse them."

Listen to Dave Clark's stream of talk:

"Now crowd in here so everybody can see this. Come right in, sir. Please, move the feet. The body will follow right along. It's called walking. Now this knife I'm going to show you, it's such a good knife, they gave us two guarantees with it. See, the handle is unbreakable. Put it in your dishwasher. The blade is highly flexible. Sword steel. Here's the sword steel trademark right on the package."

His hands move fast and so does his tongue, to hold the attention of the gathering crowd. "Did you ever watch a lady with a dull knife cut a ripe tomato? Slips and slides. If no one's looking she stabs it LIKE THIS—gives it a hemorrhage to get it going. If she's like my mother, she'll pick it up and commit hara-kiri LIKE THIS! It scares me to death.

"Now watch how this blade does the work. A lady said to me, 'Say, that's a ripe tomato. Can you cut that tomato thin?' Well, bless her stingy heart. When tomatoes are sixty-nine a pound you gotta cut thin. One tomato can last all winter with this knife.

"In forty days this knife will go on sale in stores throughout the United States and Canada for $3.98 and it's worth every penny of it. But here today, for a limited number of people, would you believe me if I told you that for only. . . . "

Little by little the crowd gets that wonderful feeling of being let in on a good thing. Dave's technique is part hypnosis, part humor, part visual aids, part carefully polished spiel. Maybe parts of his technique should be in our repertoire too.

THE JAM AUCTIONEERS

In a day of impersonalization and self-service, when customers and manufacturers bemoan the lack of friendly salespeople, the spielers appeal to human nature. It's fun to be crowding closer together, chuckling at the flow of chatter, feeling friendly toward the nice man on the platform, watching for chances to pick up a bargain.

Pitchmen who move higher-priced merchandise than the demonstrators do are called jam auctioneers. They use more elaborate plans of persuasion, but the basic ingredients are the same: humor, surprise, friendliness, lots of action to hold the attention, and the lure of free give-aways. They literally throw away dozens of gifts during the gradual warm-up for the hard sell that creeps in later.

Unless you're in the know, you can watch a good jam auction- eer at work for an hour without getting much more than a faint idea of what he's up to. And you'd better keep your hands in your pockets and concentrate on resisting hypnosis, or you may wind up as one of the many "successful" bidders.

Attracted by cries of "Free! Everybody gets one!" you see the auctioneer, a kindly, well-meaning fellow standing at a small table in front of a wide-open store or tent with neat rows of wooden chairs. He's tossing gifts into the crowd. Your first impression is that he must be an eccentric or a fool. But since everyone else is achieving the mark's dream of getting some- thing for nothing, why shouldn't you too? Your hands come out of your pockets. You grab for whatever is tossed your way. You have become a participant in his act.

Perhaps the pitchman demonstrates a plastic tube that, when stuck into an orange, lets the juice trickle out. Then he give it away. He shows and distributes other free items: a bamboo backscratcher, a potato slicer, shoelaces, a "Zippo-type" ciga- rette lighter.

But wait. He can't give lighters to anyone under eighteen. And the crowd is too large to manage. Why not have everyone move inside and sit down? Like the Pied Piper leading happy children, he shows the way into the jam joint.

There he tosses out free combs helter-skelter. "Who didn't get a lighter?" he cries, and as frantic hands stretch toward him, he thows out books of matches. Laughter swells from the crowd.

He dips into a basket and out come genuine lighters. Pens

come from another, sewing-machine needles from a third. "Relax, folks," he says. "I've enough here to go round for everyone, even if my advertising sponsors fire me for being overly generous with their products." He flings these presents far and wide.

Thus begins the process of conditioning you and his other hearers. He's given you all a dim sense of guilt. Because you're warm-hearted humans, you subconsciously want to reciprocate for the favors he's done you. You hope your gullible friend up there will sell something on which he makes at least a small profit, and thus prove to his advertising sponsors that he's not a hopeless failure. But of course nobody intends to buy any of the bigger, glistening goods on display—the wristwatches, gold clocks, AM-FM portable radios, stereo sets, sewing machines.

The pitchman isn't ready yet to start selling. You might be surprised to know that so far he has given away a total of about two dollars worth of plunder. The cigarette lighters cost him seven cents apiece. The pens wholesale at $1.50 a gross, the other items far less.

He frowns as he stares at the give-away baskets. They're empty. He shrugs in bewilderment but manfully carries on anyway. His next step is to adjust you to handing over some cash, no matter how little.

You think he'll try to auction the expensive goods you see. You feel obligated to bid at least a couple of dollars, but you're going to be mighty cautious. So is everyone else.

You all are surprised again. "For advertising," the auctioneer offers to sell a small transistor radio for fifty cents, a set of steak knives for one dollar, a camera for a dime! But only to people who will tell their friends about the superb values.

SURPRISE AFTER SURPRISE

"Let's see which people really know a value," he says, smiling. "Who'll pay three dollars for this empty box?" People enjoy his jokes. Three agree to buy.

But the boxes aren't empty. They contain gleaming gold-colored necklaces, "guaranteed not to turn color—once they're green, they stay green." The lucky ones who trusted him get necklaces, and their money back, too.

"Look at the man back there with money in his hand and tears in his eyes," jokes the auctioneer. "Never mind, sir, I'll give you another chance to prove you trust me. Now who'll pay three dollars for this bigger empty box?"

This time a score of hands shoot up. Again the boxes aren't empty. They hold ballpoint pens, stamped Gold Filigree and guaranteed "for the life of the manufacture," which all sounds impressive even if it's meaningless.

Suddenly the people who didn't buy three dollar boxes are asked to leave since they obviously aren't interested in bargains. As they go, the salesman counts the sixty dollars he took from the penbuyers, and clips some ten dollar bills to a camera, radio, and steak knives.

"Now let's see, I've obligated my advertising sponsors and myself to twenty of you good ladies and gentlemen. Let's take a look at what you're going to get. . . . But wait a minute! I almost forgot I still got more of my sponsors' free gifts to get rid of." He laughs sadly. "The boss sends spies around. Checks up on me, sees if I'm lazy and don't want to bother giving all the gifts away. Just for that I could get fired."

Shocked at the thought of such a misfortune to their over-generous friend up there, the chosen few remaining in the jam joint snatch eagerly at toothbrushes and combs thrown out from a basket in seeming profusion. (They cost the pitchman less than a cent apiece.)

"And now we can get into the auction you good folks have been waiting for so patiently. To begin, who will pay fifty cents for a ten dollar radio?" A score of hands go up. "Who'll pay $10.50 for it, just as it is?" Seeing a ten dollar bill clipped to the radio, someone timidly raises a hand and an assistant takes his money.

"There's a man who believed me when I said the radio was worth ten dollars," the pitchman says. "He trusted me. Give him back his ten dollars and just take fifty cents." He unclips the ten dollars from the radio, tucks the bill in his pocket, and passes the transistor to the happy buyer.

The camera goes to a lady for a dime. She offers $10.10, since it has ten dollars clipped to it, but the pitchman keeps his ten dollars, she keeps hers, and she gets the camera. It is the same with the steak knives.

The auctioneer scans his shelves. He chooses a box, opens it, and goggles in amazement. "Well, what do you know?" He holds up what's inside. "It's a magnificent pen and pencil set, filigreed in gold. It writes in three colors. How much does this cost, Sam?" he asks his assistant.

"Fifteen dollars," Sam answers promptly.

"Who of you will pay me a dollar for this?" There is hesitation. Only ten hands go up. "That's all who'll pay one dollar for a pen and pencil set worth at least fifteen times as much wholesale?" A few more hands go up. A dollar is taken from each "bidder," who receives a pen and pencil set. This time no money is returned.

Now for the real values. The pitchman picks up an expensive-looking electric alarm clock (worth $1.50 wholesale.) He looks at a patron who has been silent since making his first silver offering. "Would you, sir, pay me twenty-five dollars for this fabulous alarm clock worth at least fifty dollars?"

The man shakes his head.

"Would you pay me fifteen dollars?"

The mark keeps refusing until the price is down to two dollars. Then he mutters he'll buy and pulls two bills from his wallet.

"You said two dollars, sir, and you were willing to back it up. I don't want your money," the auctioneer says, astounding everyone once more. "But would you say 'thank you' if I gave you the clock?" The man says thanks and the clock is his.

Such byplay goes on until the audience (augmented by new-comers crowding in to see what the excitement is about) is thoroughly dazed. Sooner or later the auctioneer starts the "big" sales. Some of the lucky people who buy watches, radios, cameras at the low price of thirty dollars each may also get the specially priced sewing machines and stereo sets, he promises. Before long he is collecting as much as fifty-dollar payments or deposits on clocks, TV sets, "gold" cuff links, and other booty. None of this money is returned, except for occasional inter-ludes when an expensive-looking item goes for nothing more than the recipient's "thank you."

Finally a few buyers are asked which they would prefer, the sewing machine or the stereo set, "if you had your choice." The stereo has "automatic frequency control, separate tone control, a diamond stylus," and other features. "If you've priced stereos, you know they cost $200, $300, $400." He moves to the sew-ing machine. "It's by Morse, with a dial-stitch regulator and a pushbutton forward and reverse." He displays an ad to show the "nationally advertised retail price" of $319.

"Forget the price," says the pitchman. "Forget $300, or $275, or even $200. Who wants to walk out of here, the owner of this fine machine, for $160?"

Hesitantly, a couple purchase a machine without trying it. A man buys a stereo set, without hearing it, at the same price. "Sure," says the auctioneer, "we'll take your check or your credit card." The goods will be shipped to the buyers' homes by express, he promises.

Now for the cool-out, with extraction of a last few dollars. "I'd like to buy you all a drink for being such good sports but I've done all the work. Who'll give me one dollar so I can buy myself a drink?" Seven people will, amusedly, and they get bottles of perfume with twenty dollar stickers on each box. (The perfume is worth twelve cents a bottle.) To carry their trophies home, everyone gets "matched luggage," and a laugh when brown paper shopping bags are handed out. Each person also gets a good-luck pocket piece on the way out. They smile at the auctioneer. He has relieved them of $860, not counting amounts owed for items on which they've made deposits. His giveaways cost him about twelve dollars altogether.

Such hard selling is far from the $43 million hard sell that Zeckendorf gave Alcoa. But Alcoa was interested from the beginning, while a pitchman always starts with skeptical listeners. He doesn't try to hurry them as Zeckendorf did. He takes enough time to get them in good humor, win their complete attention, offer them things they want.

CAN WE LEARN FROM PITCHMEN?

When we set out to persuade a group or an individual, we must always have something to offer. It needn't necessarily be large, nor lasting, if the situation is unimportant. But it must be attractive.

Therefore, before we start, we should know exactly what inducements we intend to offer. The biggest and simplest mistakes are usually made at this stage. A would-be persuader starts talking without any clear idea of the offer he'll make. He may realize too late that he hasn't offered enough and then try to change his proposal, only to meet resistance which has hardened. Often he tries to negotiate without offering anything tangible or interesting, yet feels aggrieved when his listeners turn away.

A worse mistake is offering the wrong inducement. A hook baited with clam will catch a sea bass, but if we drop it into a trout stream we get no nibbles. So we must think about the persuadee and look at our inducement from his viewpoint, until we're sure that our bait will really attract him.

Sometimes we try to induce by threatening. This always antagonizes and usually fails. A wife may say to her husband, "If you spend another Sunday watching television, I'll take the children and leave you." At that moment he may think, "Fine, that's just what I wish you'd do."

Both parties are often surprised by the abruptness, even violence, of some failures to reach quick agreement. It's tricky enough to try to persuade a wife or husband, a friend or partner, a business prospect, a rebellious son, or a hard-boiled bureaucrat. But it's much worse to push for fast answers when trying to influence an unfriendly group—a crowd of wildcat strikers, a meeting of creditors, a surly crew, a jury.

Yet such groups are persuaded quite often. It just takes time. When it is well done, the persuadees barely feel it. Usually they think they've made their own decision unaided.

WHEN TO BE PATIENT

No difficult job of conversion can be done in haste. Few can be done in one stage, if an important issue is at stake. The biggest jobs of persuasion must be gradual, careful, and patient.

Such emotions as anger, fear, hope, and amusement lie deeper than reason. They often work against reason. So persuasion is most successful when it begins with the emotions. Before introducing any arguments, the adroit persuader begins by pleasing and flattering his prospects, reassuring them, establishing a friendly atmosphere, perhaps tantalizing them with hints and choice tidbits. Then he can begin arguing gently, watching for reactions.

How did Bismarck persuade the kings of the German states to accept an emperor over them, and to stand at his throne while he was crowned? Not just by pointing the guns of the Prussian Army at them. It was a long process, so subtle and tortuous that historians are baffled. The same is true of most diplomatic feats by Richelieu, Franklin, Disraeli, Talleyrand. We know the facts of their careers, but not how they handled their negotiations.

But these men may have some traits in common with carnival pitchmen and million dollar promoters. One is will power and concentration. If you really want to persuade people that you are the future ruler of the nation, or the proponent of an inevitably successful idea, you must first be totally determined to do so.

It helps, of course, if you believe it yourself. But you must concentrate on making others believe. Every move, every word must serve that purpose. Most people have wandering minds. If they meet someone with concentrated conviction, they are drawn into his orbit, and sooner or later they see things his way.

The missionaries who converted fierce savages and Oriental warlords were very determined, very patient. They adjusted their persuasion to the people they approached. For example, the Jesuits began the almost impossible task of converting four hundred million Chinese by studying China. They found it was ruled from the top by comparatively few men. Fine. If they could convert those few, the rest would follow eventually. Now, how could they get to the emperor, his court, and the mandarins?

By approaching them through their own interests. What interested them most? Chinese culture, especially astronomy and geography.

Therefore, the Jesuits spent years learning Chinese literature and science, making ready to win the friendship of the Chinese. After the imperial officials grudgingly admitted ten or twelve of them, the Jesuits flattered them by talking to them in their own language, and attracted them by showing specially prepared maps and astronomical instruments. ("Free gifts" again, just as the pitchman proffers.)

Instead of being expelled as foreign barbarians, they were accepted as intelligent and cultivated men. Then they delicately approached the next stage, which was to make the mandarins eager to learn from them.

They did this by talking astronomy, by making maps of the outside world with the place-names shown in Chinese characters and the Chinese capital at the center, by presenting sundials and astronomical instruments to high officials, and finally by assisting the Imperial Board of Rites to correct its calendar so as to forecast orbits and eclipses more accurately.

They had reached the point at which gradual conversion could begin.

They might well have accomplished their enormous enterprise had they not been blocked by changes of policy in the Vatican and by dynastic changes in China.

Whether they are missionaries or family men or pitchmen or promoters or politicos, nearly all successful persuaders have this much in common, I think:

First, they select an attractive inducement.

Second (or sometimes even first), they establish a welcoming atmosphere.

Third, they persuade gradually, perhaps in small doses over a long period of time, until they see that the situation is favorable.

Then, determinedly and boldly, they ride the tide to accomplishment.

Not a bad formula for any of us, is it?

7 -- *PERSUASIVE LADIES*
Strategies by the Gentler Gender

Problem: How do you persuade people to do something if they're prejudiced against you before they ever set eyes on you?

Sometimes you use a go-between, as we saw in Chapter 1. Sometimes you jolt them out of their mental rut by doing something totally unexpected, as we saw in Chapter 2.

But if you're a woman trying to earn a living in a man's world, you need a far bigger arsenal of strategies because you run into prejudice almost every hour of the day. A woman city editor, a woman lawyer, a woman financial executive must be twice as good as men, and twice as persuasive, in order to work her way through a masculine hierarchy that constantly discriminates against her.

Let's take a look at some ladies who have been successful in such work and see what we can learn from them.

My friend Mrs. Agness Sullivan Underwood, who was for years the city editor of a big daily newspaper, the Los Angeles *Herald-Express,* was above all an expert all-round newswoman. She broke in as a cub reporter in the days when reporters scorned and resented a feminine intruder. She proved she could cover a story with the best legmen and could write and edit

103

too. She never would have reached the top without a headful of journalistic expertise.

But she needed more than the technical skills of her profession. She needed magical persuasiveness. She was dealing not only with hostile male reporters from rival papers, but also with tough characters who disliked all newspaper people: police chiefs, district attorneys, prison wardens, and criminals. She had to pry the news out of such people, and keep it exclusive if she could.

In one famous case, meeting a runaway murderess as a total stranger, Aggie quickly made her a firm friend. Mrs. Hazel Glab, an attractive thirty-five-year-old blonde who had shot her husband, not only promised Aggie an exclusive interview and pictures but beat off another reporter with a rolled-up newspaper and went to Aggie's home where she helped serve dinner and wash dishes. (Afterward she gave herself up and was sent to prison.) What did Aggie do to win such cooperation?

"Mostly it was simple friendliness," she explained when I asked her:

> I sized up Mrs. Glab and guessed that she'd like to have a drink. So I offered one, and she appreciated it. When I invited her out to the house, she appreciated that even more, because she probably felt the whole world was against her at that point.
>
> But there was another angle too. People enjoy doing a favor when they can, I've found, because it gives them a warm feeling. I explained to Mrs. Glab that she was a big story for the *Herald-Express,* and that she could do me a great favor by dodging the boys from other papers. She was glad to help me. As we got into my car a reporter overtook us and tried to question her. She whacked him in the face with a newspaper, shut the car door, and away we went. When we got to the house I just treated her as a friend and made her feel at home. Naturally she talked freely.

THE MAGIC OF SYMPATHY

Notice the key to Aggie's winning ways: She put herself in the other person's place. She always tried to figure out what someone needed or wanted. With the perceptiveness that seems to come more easily to the gentler sex, she sensed that Hazel Glab ached for sympathy and friendliness, and she gave it.

Time and again this won her the cooperation, and the confidence, of people who had clammed up when others tried to needle or cajole them into talking. Once a school principal, Verlin Spencer, went berserk and shot six people for what he believed was a plot to oust him from his job. He then shot himself in the chest but missed his heart. When Aggie arrived at the prison ward of General Hospital, a crowd of reporters and photographers was outside Spencer's room. He had refused to talk to them or show his face for pictures. Somebody said, "Let Aggie go in and see him. If anybody can get him talking, she can."

She did.

She merely said to Spencer, with genuine sympathy, "I feel so very sorry for you. Is there anything I can do?" From his hospital bed he told her everything and let her bring in photographers. For years afterward he wrote to her from prison.

Another time she got an exclusive interview in jail with Leroy Drake, a nineteen-year-old who had confessed to poisoning his aunt and uncle in order to inherit their $13,000 savings. The confession had been sketchy, however, and detectives who needed more facts listened nearby as Aggie tried to persuade Drake to give details. He sullenly refused. Finally, in the effort to imagine herself in his place, she remembered her own unhappy childhood as an orphan. She said, "Leroy, you had a good home with good folks, but somehow you felt you weren't wanted, that nobody really loved you as they would their own boy. Is that it?" His face cleared, and he poured out his whole story.

ANALYZE THE OTHER FELLOW'S PROBLEM

Sometimes putting oneself in another's place is less a matter of warm emotion than of analytical thinking about what can benefit him most. Let me illustrate with a couple of exploits of Fanny Holtzmann, a Jewish girl from a large family in Brooklyn who became a hugely successful international lawyer in the entertainment field.

Producer Sam Harris was rehearsing *Jubilee,* a musical comedy that raucously kidded King George V and his Queen. In London the Lord Chamberlain unofficially asked Fanny to try to talk Harris out of these plans. But the advance rumors about the hilarious show had already given *Jubilee* a big advance sale—so how could she persuade a producer to water down a sure-fire hit?

Fanny thought the problem through from the viewpoint of Sam Harris. Then she phoned him. "Listen, dear, what are you trying to do, buck the British government? Maybe you don't want to put on a show in London ever again. . . . Listen, suppose you want to sell your lousy show to the movies, what then? Then the British are laying for you, and they'll see that the picture is banned all over the British Empire." Harris saw the light. He changed the locale of *Jubilee* to a mythical kingdom. The British were pacified. After the New York opening, the *London Daily Telegraph* reported: "Fears that the play would attempt to caricature the British royal family were dissipated, although it is rumored that extensive cuts were made at the suggestion of Washington officials." Fanny's name was never mentioned, and she got no fee. But the good will of the British gave her career a big boost.

In an earlier case she was on the opposite side. She had the job of inducing the British government not to make a formal protest to Washington about a sketch roasting King George and

Agness Underwood

Queen Mary in *As Thousands Cheer*. To accomplish this delicate task, she merely dropped one sympathetic remark to the
Earl of Cromer, the Lord Chamberlain, phrasing it in a
British way: "A protest will simply give the revue tons of publicity. And one dislikes obliging the producer to that extent."

This too was a non-fee negotiation. But the influence she
acquired on both sides of the Atlantic brought a handsome pay-
off when she decided to try to sell Noel Coward's play *Cavalcade*
to Hollywood. Coward himself was cold to the idea when she
approached him. He told her that movie scouts at the London
opening had reported the play to be nothing but a loosely strung
national newsreel, of no interest to Americans. She talked to
studio producers and they confirmed Coward's doubts.

But Fanny could see what the producers couldn't. In New
York she called up Florence Strauss, story editor of Twentieth
Century-Fox, and arranged to be seated next to the new board
chairman of the film company, E. R. Tinker, at dinner at Miss
Strauss's home a few nights later. There she swung the deal.

"Such a pity," Fanny said to Tinker over the soup, "that
Hollywood has lost *Cavalcade*."

"What do you mean, 'has lost?' " Tinker inquired. "Has
somebody else bought it?"

"Well, naturally, they'll film it in England," she said. After
some thought, Tinker allowed that this was just as well. After
all, what use was *Cavalcade* to Hollywood?

"Money," Fanny replied.

She went on, "The British sales alone would pay for the cost
of making the picture, and the rest of the world would be
velvet." She looked at Tinker and sighed sympathetically.
Within the week his studio bought *Cavalcade*. Noel Coward
cabled Fanny: "I forgive you."

Agness Underwood could be just as cerebral in influencing
others when the need arose. Once she faced the problem of
persuading attorneys to postpone putting a star witness on the
stand so that his testimony could be featured in the afternoon

Herald-Express instead of the morning papers. The witness was Harry Raymond, a vice investigator whose car had allegedly been bombed by a police detective. He was to testify for the district attorney, who planned to put him on the stand in the afternoon. This meant that the morning papers would get the sensational story. Aggie went to the district attorney and argued that Raymond, still in the hospital recovering from the bomb wounds, would make a better witness if he were brought to court in the morning after a good night's sleep. Nope, Raymond was coming to court in the afternoon.

Aggie didn't give up. She went to Dick Cantillon, the defense lawyer. "Don't you think it will be better if the D.A. puts Raymond on in the morning?" she suggested. "Then you'll have the afternoon to cross-examine him without interruption, while his testimony is fresh in the jury's minds."

Cantillon saw the point. Of course he couldn't dictate when the D.A. would call Raymond, but he could keep the preceding witness on the stand indefinitely under a leisurely cross-examination. So Dick spent the whole afternoon taking that witness back and forth through his testimony. "That question has been asked and answered," the D.A. would object, and the judge would sustain the objection, but Dick cleverly kept phrasing similar questions in different words until court adjourned for the day. So Raymond took the stand next morning, on *Herald-Express* time.

In the incidents I've mentioned you'll notice that Fanny Holtzmann, unlike Mrs. Underwood, seldom had any problem in gaining the attention of people she needed to persuade. But Fanny had no entree at all when starting her career. She dropped out of school at fourteen, got a job as file clerk in a law office, and grew so fascinated with the law that she took night courses to earn a high school diploma and eventually a law degree.

Within a few years she had a host of friends in New York theatrical circles. How did she get them? Mainly by finding ways to be helpful. As big-money salesmen know, going out of their way to do favors for all acquaintances is an important part of their career. Helpfulness makes friends who may eventually become customers, or may at least open doors to other prospects.

MAKE FRIENDS BEFORE YOU NEED THEM

Here's how Fanny Holtzmann worked her way to importance in the entertainment field.

The *Morning Telegraph* was a leading theatrical paper in those days. It always had trouble collecting money due from actors and other people in show business who bought space in the paper to advertise their talents, or sometimes just their existence. Fanny offered to try to make the collections. She opened a tiny office in the Astor Theatre Building on Broadway, and wrote charming dunning letters to all the entertainers who were in debt to the *Telegraph*, begging them to come in and see F. Holtzmann.

They flocked in, pacing and gesturing and apparently threatened by terrible disasters. Mostly it was debts that troubled them, but sometimes they had given money to someone to invest for them and wanted to get it back. Fanny knew that if she was ever to collect the *Telegraph* accounts she would have to help these confused people get their finances in order. She did and they loved it. Through them she got to meet more solvent people of the theater, and thus her clientele grew.

A network of contacts is an invaluable adjunct to persuasiveness. The best way to build such a network is by getting into circulation and lending a helping hand wherever possible. I've noticed that persuasive people of both sexes tend to be naturally friendly people with a habit of helpfulness. They do favors just for the fun of it, wherever they go. Consequently they often get help from friends when they need it. Aggie Underwood often quoted the advice of her first newspaper boss, "Your friend is also a news source. The more friends—and news sources—a reporter develops, the more valuable he is to the paper."

Natural friendliness enabled another famous newspaper woman, Florabel Muir (who later was a good friend and neighbor of mine), to get started up the ladder in Salt Lake City. Newspapers there had never employed a woman reporter and didn't intend to break precedent. For months they kept refusing to hire her. So she went to work at the Newhouse Hotel, first as a mail clerk and then as a room clerk. In these jobs she learned a lot about the city and the people in it. Finally there came a day when the Salt Lake *Herald* was short-handed. No replacements were in sight. Through her contacts she heard about it and got the job, but it was a tough job. Her assignment was to cover the sheriff's office and the county jail.

The sheriff and his staff had no use for a girl reporter. They openly advised prisoners in the jail not to talk to Florabel. You can imagine how hard it was under these conditions to get a murder suspect, for example, to open up and confide in her.

But she recalls in her memoirs: "Gradually my genuine interest in people saved my neck. I began to lay what we in the newspaper game call pipelines. People liked me and I liked them. At the end of three months I had spies working for me all over the building. . . . I went to exhaustive efforts to bring the prisoners news of their womenfolk and what was going on outside. I became the little bluebird that brought them cheer, and in spite of the hostility of the jailers it wasn't long before I was getting such human-interest interviews that my city editor began to stare with admiration."

Once, when she needed to persuade a whole jury to reach agreement soon enough for her paper's deadline, Florabel used a much subtler variation of the put-yourself-in-their-place technique. The all-male jury had been deadlocked for three days in a front-page murder trial. Florabel heard that they stood 6-4 for acquittal, and she was convinced that the defendant was innocent. How could she speed up the jury's deliberations when she couldn't even come within sight of them?

She found a way. She reasoned that these men had been away from their wives for the whole six weeks of the trial. That day while they were out to lunch she sneaked into the jury room with a large bottle of sexy perfume and spilled it under the long table around which they sat and argued.

As she says in her memoirs, "The room reeked with the odor, reminding these married men of the little women waiting at home. Within an hour they reached a verdict. The judge had quite a little to say to me about the incident in the privacy of his chambers, but it was difficult to prove that I had done this intentionally when I swore I had dropped the bottle out of my purse accidentally. I had taken care to break the bottle against the leg of the table to make it look like an accident."

Another persuasive, sympathetic, and successful lady in an entirely different field is my friend Ivy Baker Priest. She was Treasurer of the United States during the Eisenhower administration, and later was twice elected State Treasurer in California. Like the other ladies I've mentioned, Mrs. Priest faced a bleak future in her youth. Two weeks after she entered the University of Utah, her father was seriously injured in an accident and she had to leave college and find a job.

Since she lacked training or experience, there weren't many jobs open to her. Still, girls could work for the telephone company, so she applied there and was hired. She might have stayed there all her life, but she dreamed of bigger accomplishments. She figured that telephone training might help her in other fields. She learned to develop a "voice with a smile" (it has enhanced her persuasiveness ever since) and used it to talk herself into a somewhat better job as a salesgirl at the Auerbach store in Salt Lake City. There she learned that "the customer is always right"—another useful attitude, as we've seen, in any work involving selling or negotiating or persuading.

PERSUASIVENESS COMES WITH PRACTICE

She also went into politics, starting at the bottom, of course, ringing doorbells as a Republican party worker. She knew it would give her valuable experience in meeting and talking with people. How right she was. Steadily improving her human-relations skills, Ivy worked her way upward in both merchandising and politics. She became a buyer and then an executive for Auerbach and later for Bullock's Wilshire in Los Angeles. Meanwhile, she also served ten years as a member of the Republican National Committee, finally becoming its assistant chairman in charge of women's organizations during the 1952 presidential campaign.

Along the way she made a national reputation by helping the party elect Republicans to many minor offices which had been held for decades by Democrats. Her bright-eyed smile and enthusiastic voice made people want to participate in the hard unpaid labor of campaigning. "To capture the White House we start with the courthouses," she kept saying, and the organization she helped build was the proof of the theory. Eisenhower's victory in 1952 was the first time the Republicans had captured the White House in twenty-four years.

Soon after the election, the grateful new President telephoned to ask her to become U.S. Treasurer. She knew little about governmental finance and wondered whether she should attempt the job. "Nothing has ever been easy for me," she said. But she told herself, "Ike wouldn't have asked me unless he were sure I could do it." So she went to Washington to take charge of a staff of sixty-five civil service workers, mostly male.

She had no trouble getting their cooperation because she wasn't bossy. Instead of issuing orders, she made suggestions and requests. In the rare cases where this didn't work, she simply explained the reasons for her request and kept following up to make sure it was carried out.

The toughest test of her persuasiveness came early. Hard-boiled efficiency experts from the powerful General Services Administration proposed to rearrange her whole section of the Treasury Department building. This meant junking a new million dollar switchboard in order to "save valuable space." They obviously considered the Treasurer an unimportant figure-head and took no heed of her objections.

STRATEGY FOR SHOWDOWNS

When confronted by completely closed minds, the best strategy is usually to appeal to a higher authority who is likely to be open-minded. For some reason women seem to do this better than men, perhaps because they run into such situations so often. In her confrontation with the GSA, Ivy finally tele-phoned the Secretary of the Treasury. "I'm a former telephone operator," she began—a humble opening which reassured him that she wasn't about to make imperious demands—"and I'd like to offer some suggestions for your consideration, about the telephone facilities here." She had no trouble convincing him that her ideas were more sensible than the changes planned by the GSA men.

Women are generally expected to be submissive in the busi-ness and professional world. They get lower salaries and fewer promotions. Sometimes submissiveness is good strategy for a while. But occasionally a woman must seek a showdown rather than let men trample all over her. Let's see how such crises have been handled by the ladies I've been discussing.

Once Agness Underwood went to Inglewood to cover a big murder investigation, only to encounter a self-important police chief who brushed aside her questions. She chose a moment for a showdown when his men, and other police from neighboring jurisdictions, were present. "All right now, chief," she snapped, "are you going to hold still long enough to answer reasonable questions, or are you going to act like just another hick-town cop?" The men laughed in his face and he agreed to give twice-daily briefings. How could he refuse?

The same sort of challenge worked well at other times when Aggie could get no help from some cop on a beat. She would say something like, "Look, mister, you may be sore at me because I'm a reporter, or you may be just sore at the world. I'm not doing anything to you. But you're doing something to me with this damned stalling. I don't want to do anything to hurt you." (Notice the veiled threat.) "You seem to think you're out here because you're in bad. Don't make it worse. Let's get along. What do you say?" Usually her plea succeeded.

BLOCKED? GO HIGHER

When sweet reason failed, Aggie would get the man's superior on the phone if she could. The higher-up was usually a friendly acquaintance of hers and knew the importance of press relations better than underlings did. This forthright tactic of going over the head of the mulish opponent is one which many successful women use in emergencies.

For example, Adela Rogers St. Johns, another famous reporter, often ran into opposition from woman-hating executives in the Hearst organization, for which she worked. In such cases she challenged them to telephone William Randolph Hearst himself at San Simeon. The challenge was almost always accepted, and Hearst would almost invariably rule in Adela's favor. She knew how his mind worked.

During World War II, when military planes crashed frequently in the Los Angeles area and it was up to the newspapers to get the story, Agness Underwood often had trouble with rank-happy officers who wanted to show how stern and secretive they could be. Even stray sergeants began to prevent news photographers from getting pictures of wrecked planes. But Aggie knew the security regulations better than the officers did. (Being meticulously well-informed and well-prepared is a big help in a showdown of any kind.) She challenged them to go to a telephone with her and call the military public-relations office. Many a time she briskly recited the regulations over the phone, for the benefit of an officious sergeant or lieutenant standing by, then handed the phone to him and heard him "Yes Sir"-ing until his face was red.

Careful preparation paid off for Fanny Holtzmann in a showdown in England. Tex Austin's rodeo had been booked as an attraction at the Wembley Exhibition, but Tex was worried about the possible reaction of animal-loving Englishmen to the rigors of a rodeo. He asked Fanny to represent him. Sure enough, the Royal Society for the Prevention of Cruelty to Animals haled him into court.

Fanny produced a brief crammed with facts she had absorbed in the New York Public Library about cowboys, steers, the Wild West, and the policies of the SPCA in America. It was all pretty astounding to British ears. The court ruled in favor of the rodeo and it prospered at Wembley, helped by the newspaper publicity given the case.

Sometimes, of course, there is no higher officialdom which can be invoked against arbitrary and unfair opposition. In such crises, successful women have used widely varying tactics. Red-headed Florabel Muir, after being baited for a month by a foul-mouthed reporter from an opposition newspaper, suddenly threw her typewriter at him and swore she would kill him. He fled from the pressroom and never bothered her again.

Facing rather similar bullying during her first assignment in a courtroom, Aggie Underwood defied it more quietly. A quarrelsome, high-handed reporter challenged her when she tried to take a seat in the press row. She showed her press card but he wasn't at all satisfied. "Get back to the society page," he snarled. "You don't belong here. Your paper will send down a regular reporter."

Aggie simply sat down in the press section. He couldn't very well pull her out of her seat. Other reporters did try to get a bailiff to eject her but the bailiff laughed at them.

Ivy Baker Priest quietly absorbed a bawling-out from Fred Auerbach, owner of the store for which she worked, one day when he was in an ornery mood and disliked an idea she had submitted. Finally she said quietly, "You must have had some confidence in me or you wouldn't have put me in this job." He stopped pacing, turned and stared at her, then said, "You're right." In a softer voice he went on to discuss her idea more reasonably and eventually okayed it.

KIDDING CAN BE BETTER THAN CONFRONTATION

When Ivy was in Washington, her Assistant Treasurer was another remarkable woman, Catherine Cleary. An outgoing woman with a keen sense of humor, she has her own prescription for persuading unfriendly people to change: "I think you have to do this by kidding people along. I don't believe in confrontation—or not for myself, anyway. The greatest thing is example."

Miss Cleary is now president of First Wisconsin Trust Company, which manages $1.25 billion in assets. Strange as it seems, the Milwaukee Estate Planning Council has never opened its doors to women, thus depriving her of membership even though she heads the largest trust company in Wisconsin. But she accepts this discrimination peaceably. She seems to get along very well with most businessmen, for she is a member of the board of directors of General Motors, A. T. & T., and several other corporate giants. Why should she seek a showdown over membership in one Milwaukee organization?

When you come to think of it, many showdowns and confrontations can be avoided with just as good results in the long run. Maybe we should all laugh more often when someone frustrates us.

8 -- FROM TIN CUPS TO TELETHONS

Persuading People to Donate

A few years ago I found myself on the receiving end of a fund-raising campaign which was so persuasive that I not only contributed money but ended up giving my time to persuade other people to contribute.

The campaign was for Springfield College, one of hundreds of small private religious colleges in chronic need of money. Unlike most, Springfield was remarkably adroit in going after donations. That's why I want to tell you about it.

One of its fund-raising campaigners happened to notice a fact about me which was mentioned somewhere in print: As a young man I had wanted to become a YMCA athletic director and had wanted to attend Springfield College because it was founded for the purpose of training "Y" workers. I never got there because I couldn't afford it; since I lived in San Diego I worked my way through San Diego State College instead. Nevertheless, the scrap of information about my sole, fragile link with Springfield was clipped, filed away, and acted on in due time. I was invited to the college to receive an honorary degree. Springfield wished to honor me not only because of my achievements,

I was told, but because of my youthful desire to study there. It was a nice sentimental touch.

Even though recognizing honorary degrees as bait for donations, few people decline one. I went to Massachusetts as if extradited. When the reception committee showed me around the campus, there still wasn't even a hint of a request for money. But the committee made sure I got an eyeful of the college swimming pool, which was one of the smallest, shabbiest, and oldest I'd seen at any institution of higher learning. The Springfield people knew that swimming was one of my favorite sports. They had even dug up the fact that I won a Southern California backstroke championship when I was a boy at the San Diego "Y." They mentioned this fact, as I gazed at their forlorn swimming pool, and we naturally drifted into quite a chat about swimming. You can guess the outcome. I eventually offered to contribute the cost of a new and better pool.

My relationship didn't end there. Springfield was too smart for that. Its administrative people showed such real appreciation of my gift, and such admiration for the financial acumen they seemed to think I possessed, that I found myself giving them advice on financial problems when they asked for it. From there it was only a step to joining the fund-raising committee myself.

I guess I must have realized, even before I agreed to serve, that I was taking on the toughest job of money-seeking I'd ever tackled. I've helped raise large sums for a wide variety of charities: I've been national chairman of the Easter Seal drive for crippled children, the Heart Fund drive, and the Arthritis Foundation drive; I've made a movie for the World Vision International; I've served on national campaign committees for Good Will Industries, for the Foster Parents Plan for War Orphans, and of course for the YMCA; and I've helped with a bunch of telethons, and about umpty-nine hundred charity banquets. In fact, the first public appearances of my life were made in a fund-raising capacity, walking down a church aisle as a small boy, passing a collection plate at the church where my father was minister. But none of these chores compared in difficulty with the Springfield College problem.

Here was an almost unknown, totally unglamorous school. Its athletic teams were never on TV. Its professors were seldom asked for advice in Washington. It's alumni weren't in the society columns or the business headlines. How could I ask people in California or New York to give money to this small Massachusetts college when so many colleges in their own states were pulling old school ties? So many worthy organizations, inside and outside of the educational field, needed money so badly that there couldn't possibly be enough charity dollars to go around. In some cities the residents were (and still are) exposed to six hundred national fund-raising campaigns and more than a thousand local drives per year—an average of four solicitations daily. How could Springfield buck such massive competition?

Well, we did buck it. And I'm proud to report that we raised $7.5 million.

HOW A SMALL COLLEGE RAISED BIG MONEY

The ways we did it may be useful to know when you go out to raise money for charity—which nearly everyone does from time to time, since this is one of the implied responsibilities of American citizenship.

I think three factors enabled us to put over the Springfield drive: 1) we did our homework in advance, 2) we hunted for prospects who would have personal reasons for giving, and 3) we showed what a gift would accomplish.

These are fundamentals in the art of persuading people to give generously to a worthy cause. Let's consider them.

As I mentioned, Springfield had noted and filed some pertinent facts about me, and about many other people. This was part of the necessary homework. It also compiled lists of all

Springfield alumni and their current whereabouts, if known; of all people who had previously contributed money to Springfield, and the amounts; and of all people who might have a personal reason for giving, such as a family connection or an interest in YMCA training, which was Springfield's semi-unique specialty.

Do you begin to see that a fund-raising campaign resembles a sales campaign? In each case the first step is to scan the horizon for the likeliest prospects. The next step is to figure out the sales talk, which may be different for each type of prospect.

Our sales talks for Springfield fitted an axiom of fund-raisers: "The cause and the need are bigger than the institution." In other words, you don't ask people to give money to the community hospital, but to help the health of the community; not to support the Boys' Club or the YMCA but to provide wholesome recreation for youth. You show contributors that their gifts will make things happen. You tell previous contributors exactly what their money accomplished last time, and you tell new prospects what it could do this time.

So instead of merely asking that people give to Springfield because it was a needy college, we had to show how their gifts would be meaningful. Here's what we did.

We pointed out to prospects who had put themselves through school, or had received scholarships they'd badly needed, that a gift of a scholarship "would give a young man a chance to make his own way, as you did." We reminded other prospects that money for buildings or equipment would really be money spent to produce youth workers and social workers who'd keep people off relief rolls and out of jails and hospitals; dollars at Springfield would mean fewer dollars needed for taxes everywhere.

Wherever we could possibly make a personal visit to a prospect, or could get someone else to, we didn't rely on mail appeals or phone calls. An appeal by circular or letter is the easiest to ignore, because the recipient figures that countless other people got the same mailing—and because even when a recipient in-

Art Linkletter

tends to respond, he may never get around to doing so. We all know how many low-priority letters are lost forever in the mountains of paper that pile up around the house.

A phone call is the next easiest to turn down, because people think "It can't be very important if he's doing nothing more strenuous than picking up the phone." A casual approach in asking for money can be casually evaded.

But when you take the trouble to go and see someone personally, he knows it's important to you. He can't easily say No while you're looking him in the eye. Of course he may stall if you give him the chance; he may say, "Sure, leave the pledge card. I'll think it over and figure out how much I can give." If a prospect won't fill out the card on the first visit, successful solicitors take it away with them and promise to return later.

THREE C'S SPELL SUCCESS

I've heard these fundamentals of fund raising summed up another way by campaigners who say, "Drives succeed because of three C's: Coverage, Communication, and Conversation." Coverage means good lists of people to be asked for contributions and solicitors who will do the asking. Communication means telling a good sales story. Conversation is the face-to-face contact between volunteer worker and prospective donor that cashes in on the coverage and communication.

The communication and conversation work best when they occur between people who know each other and are more or less equals. A corporation president is the best man to solicit another corporation president. Justin W. Dart, president of Dart Industries (which used to be the Rexall Drug organization), is one of America's highest-powered volunteer money-raisers because he personally goes out to other presidents' homes on Sundays and puts the arm on them. By the same token, suppose you answer a knock on your door and see one of your neighbors; he reminds you about a fire at his house last year, when the volunteer fire department saved his son's life and kept the fire from spreading. He wants to make sure the neighbors respond to the fund drive for the fire department. You dig down in your pocket, because his man-to-man appeal makes your support seem important.

Knowing this, I went out to talk with my own friends about Springfield. I tackled my easiest prospects first, as any salesman tries to do. This built up my experience and enthusiasm, besides giving me a list of donors I could mention to other prospects.

Naturally I ran into sales resistance, because my friends knew little or nothing about the college. I was ready with my sales story about the good that their gifts would accomplish. And I had answers for some objections I anticipated. When someone said, "I prefer to give to charities here in Los Angeles," I was forearmed with a list of Springfield graduates who were helping to run charitable agencies in Los Angeles. "These fellows are spending your charity dollars right here," I said. "They were trained at Springfield. You can understand why we need such well-trained pros at the head of the YMCA and the other social agencies you support. You don't want amateurs running those organizations, any more than you want amateurs running your business. Crime is up in Los Angeles—which costs you money —because kids are getting into trouble. We need more and better social workers to get them off the streets. Now, here's what your gift to Springfield can mean to Los Angeles. . . ." If you'll pardon the expression, it was a touching performance.

I also had friends in Pittsburgh. When Pittsburghers told me, "Our charity money must be spent in Pittsburgh," they spoke with strong conviction. But I'd figured out an answer in advance.

"Great!" I told them. "We'll use your money to send a Pittsburgh boy to Springfield College. Let's see, one scholarship will cost— " It worked.

NAME YOUR FIGURE

In the Springfield drive, as in other successful ones, we tried to be ready with specific suggestions about how much an individual should give. It's a mistake to say "Give what you'd like to." This leads to sad surprises—a five dollar contribution, maybe, from someone who could spare one hundred dollars. People seldom give important money without being asked specifically for it. If a respected friend aims high in his request, they're likely to respond.

This was a hard principle for me to grasp. I used to gulp before telling someone I thought he should give $5,000 or $500 or $50, if that was the amount I figured him for. Maybe you'll find it hard, too. But when you try it, you'll be surprised to find that people never resent being told that they are thought to be among the top 10 percent of the prospects, or that their net worth and their generosity have been rated high. Oh, they often scream, "I don't have that kind of money!" but they're secretly pleased anyhow, and if you make them see why the money is needed and what it can do, they'll probably have that kind of money after all.

Motivation researchers have discovered that people feel secretly uneasy when approached by a charity solicitor, because they don't know how much they ought to give. By an odd quirk of human nature, they don't want to look cheap—nor foolishly extravagant either—in the eyes of even a strange solicitor. They would like to measure up to his image of them if they can. So if he shows them a chart indicating how much is usually given by similar people (one day's pay, or a stated percentage of yearly income, or some other fair-share standard) they will probably give more than if they'd had no guidance. This is a principle known to all expert fund-raisers.

The principle applies much more commandingly when you go after big gifts. Every major prospect on your list should be approached by someone who knows him well enough to estimate how much to ask for. Businessmen are usually good at this kind of solicitation. They know each other and they know where the money is and they don't have to go hat in hand or hesitantly, as a stranger might.

ELOQUENCE ISN'T ESSENTIAL

Fortune once estimated that the average top-level business executive spends anywhere from five to fifteen hours each week raising money for worthy causes. Only a few such men have any personal background in sales work. Most of them came up through finance, engineering, or production. Consequently, they're not likely to be spellbinding persuaders in the manner of a Glenn Turner or Charles Luckman or Herbert Bayard Swope. Yet they do bring in the gifts. Which goes to show that dazzling techniques aren't needed to raise money for a worthwhile cause. All that's needed is to go out and talk to people and convince them with deep seriousness.

For example, Jesse Tapp, the retired board chairman of the huge Bank of America, never came across as a forceful, persuasive tycoon. People meeting him as strangers were apt to put him down as a former teacher or farmer, both of which he had been. Yet in his mild unobtrusive way, for many years after he left the bank and no longer was anyone to be reckoned with in business, Jesse kept on raising big sums for the National 4-H Foundation, the Boy Scouts, the Los Angeles Community Chest, and Occidental College. He once explained how he did it: "I just keep talking about what we want to do until they ask me how much it's going to cost."

However, there are some big businessmen, forceful by nature, who set out to raise money through sheer intimidation. Often they get what they demand, especially from those who have business reasons to fear them—but they also offend a lot of others who might give money if approached more diplomatically. Let me cite a few examples of what I consider the wrong way to wring gifts from prospects.

GIVE—OR ELSE?

Back when movie studios were enormous and powerful, the head of a big studio once invited me to his home to meet a new U.S. Senator. About ten other people in show business were there, too. We enjoyed chatting with the guest of honor across the dinner table and listening to a short talk by him afterward. But then our host rose and said, "Gentlemen, you've met our new Senator and I'm sure you're favorably impressed. The purpose of this meeting is to raise funds for his next campaign. I want each of you in turn to stand up and announce how much you will contribute. We'll start with you, Art."

He was copying the technique of the famous "calling dinners" which kick off major Jewish charity campaigns. At these dinners the chairman calls the roll and each guest rises when his name is called. The chair challenges each in turn: "All right Jack, what will you give? Don't be cheap. . . . Morris, you gave $25,000 last time, make it more this time." It's brutal but it works—maybe because all those present are good friends, all are enthusiastic about the charity they'll be asked to support. All these essential conditions were lacking at the movie mogul's dinner. His crudity in twisting my arm made me mad enough to disregard his influence in the entertainment world.

So I stood up and said, "I had no idea when I came to dinner that I would be asked for money. I've just met our Senator for the first time. I like him. I'll probably vote for him when the time comes. But it's too early for me to be sure. Before I contribute to any candidate's campaign fund, I want to know a lot more about him than I know about the Senator as of now." And I sat down. The others all stood up and promised handsome contributions, because they knew they had to. But I'll bet they never gave the Senator another dime voluntarily.

Another time a newspaper executive sent me a blunt letter asking for a specified four-figure sum to beautify the landscape by planting trees. I wrote back to the effect that while I was in favor of green landscapes and their ecological implications, I still considered people more important than trees and was putting all the money I could afford into charities that helped people. Back came another curt note: "I see I was remiss in not making clear how important these trees are to me personally. When may I expect your contribution?"

It was another barefaced attempt at bullying, this time through the power of the press, which is supposed to be all-important to entertainers. But I had survived a boycott by the Hearst newspapers early in my career. William Randolph Hearst blamed me when a man in my studio audience unexpectedly spouted anti-Hearst remarks over the air. For two years thereafter my name was not mentioned in any Hearst newspaper and Hearst radio logs did not list my programs. That hurt all right but it didn't kill my career. So no newspaper scares me now. I again declined to pay for planting trees unless the publishing executive would contribute an equal sum to one of my favorite charities. I heard nothing further. The executive has ignored me at a few parties since then, which sometimes gets a bit awkward for all concerned, but I don't lose any sleep over it.

Another tough, stupid, and widely resented campaign to get donations was carried on by a high executive of one of the big aircraft companies. Each year he wrote to the company's suppliers and subcontractors all over the country, calling for contributions to a local youth agency of which he was an enthusiastic backer. Since he wrote on his company's letterhead and signed his company title, the message was clear: Contribute to my charity or you may lose a big customer.

I don't know how much money he brought in, plenty,

probably. But it was bad for the company and bad for the youth agency. Sometimes a corporation needs friends. When this company needed them it had none. Nobody lifted a finger to ease some painful shortages of cash and materials which put the company in jeopardy. So the company no longer exists. As for the youth organization, it merged with another one and moved its headquarters to a different city.

I'm convinced that tact is better than toughness, even in solo face-to-face solicitations. I'll grant that the tactful solicitor doesn't always bring in as much as the bully—but sometimes he brings in more, when he asks for it, and he makes fewer enemies for himself and his charity. We all remember the guy who tries to browbeat us. I'll never forget one major industrialist who came to my house to solicit funds for the Republican party, of which I happen to be an enthusiastic supporter. I told him I would contribute a certain sum. He laughed as if I'd said something hilarious, then gave me a hard stare. "Come on, come on, Art! You can afford five times that much. Listen to how much these other guys gave." He quoted names and sums. Then he mentioned sneeringly the names of some "little guys" who in spite of their littleness had given somewhat bigger sums than I proposed to give.

Again the message was plain. He would be telling my friends just how much I donated. This is an ugly kind of pressure, even when no friends are involved. It's human nature not to want anyone to consider you cheap, especially when you're in the same room with him. That's why very few of us walk out of a restaurant without leaving a sizable tip, no matter how surly the service is. When a forceful person implies that you're a jerk or a tightwad, that your acquaintances behave better than you do, and that they'll be informed of your delinquency—well, it's embarrassing, sure enough.

But I guess I'm hard to embarrass, having coped with so many difficult situations during radio and television shows. If a corporation president chooses to spread around an accusation that I'm miserly, it doesn't bother me much because most people who know me are aware of some things I've done for various charities. In the case of this Republican fund-raiser, I think he might have talked me into giving more if he'd given me better reasons for contributing, instead of trying to shame me. Anyhow, I'll probably be out next time he calls. Hereafter I'll send my contributions to the Grand Old Party through other channels.

HOW WE CHOOSE

We're all bombarded with requests for financial help. We can't respond to every appeal, even if we happen to be named Rockefeller or Ford. We're forced to pick and choose. What makes us choose this cause or that project?

We give most amply to whichever ones we can be made to care about and believe in, especially if we see their needs as urgent. So the art of persuading people to donate consists mostly in painting two vivid, convincing pictures—one picture of a situation that needs changing, and another picture of the changes that can happen when people donate.

Probably you had two such pictures in your mind when you undertook to raise funds for any worthy cause. Otherwise you wouldn't voluntarily have undertaken the assignment. The pictures may have been clear in your mind because of your own first-hand, on-the-scene knowledge. (If not, perhaps you should do a little leg work; go out and look at whatever you're raising money for. Then you can talk about it more convincingly.) Anyhow, your job is to put pictures into the minds of prospective donors. Maybe photographs or posters can do this job. Maybe just a word picture will do it, especially when backed up by a startling fact or two, such as "There are seventeen million victims of arthritis—one of every eleven Americans." "In our community roughly 70 percent of the boys aged sixteen to twenty-one are unemployed." "Dangerous drugs can be bought openly any evening on the Harvard Common."

Solid facts are needed to clinch your selling job. But they seldom do the job alone. They must be dramatized. People are interested in people, less interested in abstractions or statistics. So when you want to raise money, tell true stories about people, and show pictures of people if you can. People give far more to other people than to any vague "worthy cause."

When I took on a big job of fund raising for the World Vision International, I went to Saigon and followed a street boy for a day with camera and microphone. Then I did the same with a Chinese fishing boy in Hong Kong finally and; with a Korean orphan who had been left to die on a garbage dump eighteen years earlier. The eye remembers what the ear forgets, as I've stressed elsewhere in this book, and those moving pictures of orphans really did move people. The narration reinforced the pictures with human-interest information that couldn't be photographed, such as the nonexistence of schooling or medicine for these kids. The big trip-hammer fact went into the sub-title: *A Billion and Three.* Approximately a billion children are in the terrible position of the three we pictured.

SALES TALK FOR AN ORPHAN

Now let's assume you too are raising funds for World Vision, but there's no movie to help you. Your main tool is your tongue. What can you say?

You might begin as I sometimes do: "How would you like to adopt a child? You can do it for only fifty cents a day—fifteen dollars a month."

The most arresting word in the language is "you." If you use this word a couple of times in your first two sentences, you'll grab your listener. If you combine this with a surprising idea, he'll listen more closely. Of course he isn't about to adopt a child literally, but the sheer strangeness of the idea, combined with the surprising figures about the small cost, will hold him momentarily. Now you must show him you're serious.

You continue: "Fifteen dollars is hardly cigarette money for you—but it will buy food, medicine, care, and clothing for a Korean orphan for a month." The idea is to talk about somebody specific whenever you can. At this point you might show a snapshot of the Korean child.

Soon it will be time for a change of pace, bringing "you" in once more:

"Do you have any children? Here's a way you can impress on your children how lucky they are. Let them become pen pals with your new foster child in Korea. They will have the letters translated and read to her. Then her reply will be translated and sent back. Wouldn't your children like to take this correspondence to school and share it with their own schoolmates?" And so on. As every salesman knows, you must show your prospect how he benefits before he'll part with any money. The World Vision people can be more specific than most charities, which sometimes can offer only the intangible but pleasant feeling anyone gets when he helps someone else. Often this is enough. Normal people get pleasure from giving.

If you raised an eyebrow at that last sentence, just stop and ponder some facts. Out of the goodness of their hearts, more than fifteen million people contributed their time as amateur fund-raisers in 1954, and they persuaded other people to donate a total of $5,400,000,000—yes, $5.4 billion! By 1963 there were about fifty million of us working for free on behalf of charities, and we brought in more than $10 billion. In 1968, the latest year for which the Internal Revenue Service has detailed breakdowns, individual Americans gave something over $11.1 billion to worthy causes. This total happened to be the equivalent of two-thirds of all the dividends paid during the year by companies listed on the New York Stock Exchange. In other words, you might say that charitable giving is one of America's major industries.

A solid percentage of people give cash to anyone who rattles a cup in the streets or passes a hat in a crowd. Every news story about someone in unusual trouble is followed by unsolicited donations in the next mail. Even when it's just a joke, any appeal for charity brings in some money. A San Diego sports announcer, Rod Page, was only kidding when he suggested on his radio show that a "Dollars for Duane" drive be launched on behalf of a disgruntled professional football player, Duane Thomas, who was earning only $20,000 a year and was holding out for $100,000. Duane wasn't exactly impoverished, yet donations poured in so bountifully that a committee had to be organized at the radio station to return the money to the donors.

It was in *Reader's Digest,* I think, that I read of a pick-up man for a service that cleaned Venetian blinds. He learned not to say "I'm here for the Venetian blind" when he went to a house, because too often a bemused but charitable householder pressed some money into his hand and turned away. That's how people are. When asked, they often give, even if they have only the foggiest notion of what they're giving to.

This fact is worth remembering if you ever help to plan a mass solicitation. Try to get lots of solicitors out ringing doorbells or even appealing to pedestrians on the sidewalks. They'll raise money in direct proportion to the number of people they ask. It's a mathematical certainty.

Mathematics make telethons the most potent of all fund-raising devices. Whatever appears for a stretch of several hours on TV is seen by millions of people. And if you ask a million people for donations, several thousand are sure to respond. One Jerry Lewis nationwide telethon for muscular dystrophy brought in about 300,000 pledges and raised more than $8 million.

TIPS FOR TELETHONERS

People with very little experience but lots of good connections sometimes stage a telethon. They are moderately successful, but they fall far short of the amounts they could raise with expert management. Just in case you're ever involved in organizing one of these massive shows, here are a few pointers that may help your group multiply its pulling power. (My authority for much of the following is Jack Rourke, known as King of the Telethons because his Burbank studio has produced twenty-five successful ones in the last fifteen years.)

Your group should figure on working almost night and day for a full two months before the air date. The earliest steps are to get a permit from your city social service commission to do the telethon; get clearance from the theater authority (which represents all theatrical unions except the musicians) so that stars can appear without pay; and persuade a television station to broadcast the program without charging for its air time.

Picking a good date for your telethon is all-important. It must not conflict with any other big event—either a major TV special that might draw off most of your audience, or some other benefit show such as a celebrity golf tournament that would tie up many of the stars you hope to get on your show.

After you've arranged the necessary clearances and set the date, the next step is to program the nineteen or twenty-four hours or whatever period your show will be on the air. This is where inexperienced organizers fall down. They get promises from entertainers without any clear understanding about the time schedule. The result is that stars drop in at the studio on the way to a dinner party, on the way home, between shooting sessions of a movie, or whenever else happens to suit them. They all expect to be put on the air promptly. But one comedian won't follow another; a singer with a happy song doesn't want to appear right after a sad picture of the victims of a calamity. Conflicts are inevitable. Confusion reigns.

You can't blame show people for being particular about the conditions of their charity appearances, since they're giving away the only thing they have to sell—their talent—and they don't want to hurt their careers with a poorly-received appearance. They also lead crowded lives and resent being kept waiting indefinitely. At one telethon Sammy Davis stood around for two hours before his patience gave out and he left without ever being presented. Many other stars would have departed sooner.

To avoid all this pain and strain, seasoned producers like Rourke work out a schedule for the entire telethon in fifteen-minute segments. They find out, weeks in advance, what time will be convenient for a performer and put him on the schedule for that time. He receives a letter confirming the time, enclosing a parking pass (another troublesome detail often overlooked), and a leaflet of information about the charity for which the telethon will be staged. He is asked to arrive at the studio about thirty minutes in advance for make-up and briefing. Rourke always has some musical groups standing by to fill in when a performer doesn't arrive on schedule.

Another important part of the preparations is to recruit the girls who will answer the phones and tally the pledges from viewers. Rourke usually gets a group of airline stewardesses, since their training makes them polite and poised under pressure. He gives each girl a mimeographed sheet of instructions. Here are part of the instructions for the annual "Stop Arthritis" telethon:

Answer the phone "Stop Arthritis Telethon, your name and address please." Then, "Your phone number and the amount you want to pledge?"
Please fill out the forms as you receive the information.

The completed forms will be picked up by the collectors continuously.

Look busy at all times.

Please don't chat on the calls. Make them brief so that more people can get in. If a caller is difficult, be pleasant, don't argue, hang up.

Don't accept any collect calls.

At the end of each call, please say: "Thank you and please mail your pledge to Arthritis, Box 7, Los Angeles 51." (IMPORTANT)

Systematic follow-through makes a big difference. At Rourke's telethons, an operator immediately calls back anyone who phones in a pledge of twenty-five dollars or more to verify that the call was genuine. (A few drunks and sick jokesters like to call in fake pledges, but they never give their true phone numbers.) A few days later everyone who pledged will receive a reminder by mail, together with a return envelope for sending in the check. These little reminders are fitted with a carbon sheet, so that a second follow-up card is typed at the same time. The second card goes out in a month or so, to those who haven't yet fulfilled their pledge. You may be surprised to know that the total eventually received will surpass the total of pledges shown on the big "tote board" during the show. Not only do almost all who pledge make good on it, but many others who couldn't get through the jammed switchboard will send in checks anyway. A trickle of money continues for as long as six months after a well-run telethon.

THE POWER OF APPRECIATION

Whether you help to run a big telethon or small club's fund-raising drive, or anything in between, remember that people secretly crave recognition. You should say thanks publicly to everyone who works on your drive or who contributes to it. Hence the paper poppies which veterans' organizations stick in your lapel; the "We Gave" stickers for windows; the engraved certificates and wall plaques and desk statuettes.

Beyond this, a donor likes to see his name in print and his picture in the paper. Therefore the most successful drives arrange for local newspapers to print the names of people who give sizable amounts, and send a photographer to take pictures of big donors in the act of handing over a check.

Some organizations, notably churches and schools, even publish booklets listing their supporters. The "Century Club," an honorary organization of those who give one hundred dollars or more, is a feature of some campaigns.

Corporations, too, cherish symbols of achievement. If you're old enough you'll remember that many workers, from factory managers down to the assembly lines, moved mountains during World War II for the right to fly the Navy's "E" banner on the factory flagpole. Today they'll strive almost as hard for some bauble which betokens their civic-mindedness. I remember a striking example of this in Long Beach, California.

For years the Long Beach Community Chest had awarded a plastic plaque (which looked like bronze) to firms which met a certain standard of fair-share giving. The standard must have been hard to meet; in fourteen years only fifteen plaques were earned. But in 1960 the solicitors talked it up when they approached business executives. The result was amazing. Before the 1960 campaign was fully under way, thirty-six firms qualified for plaques.

One Long Beach furniture store sent in money and pledges which were only twelve dollars short of the amount required for a plaque. A Chest worker phoned the owner to thank him for his good showing and sympathize with him on missing the award so narrowly. The furniture man snapped, "I'm coming over." Fifteen minutes later he strode into the Chest office with a twelve dollar check, thereby winning a plaque which cost less than a dollar.

AIM FOR THE HEART

"The heart has many reasons which reason never knows," wrote Blaise Pascal, who was a profound philosopher as well as an eminent scientist. If your target is a man's pocketbook, start shooting at his heart, not his head. The administrators of New York's Columbia-Presbyterian Medical Center knew this when they decided to ask General Lucius D. Clay to head their fund-raising drive; they knew that he had undergone two serious operations there, and was profoundly grateful to the hospital for restoring him to health. Because his heart was in the drive, General Clay exerted all his immense talents and energy, and raised $50 million for the hospital.

When the New York Philharmonic needed money, it likewise did some detective work to find a big business executive whose heart was tugged by classical music. It discovered that David Keiser, board chairman of the Cuban-American Sugar Company, had been a Juilliard School student and had given up a chance for a concert career because his father needed him in the sugar company. He was still such a brilliant amateur pianist that the Philharmonic could appropriately invite him to join Leonard Bernstein in several performances of a Bach concerto at Carnegie Hall. From then on the Philharmonic was Keiser's great hobby, and he became its dynamic president, as well as a generous financial supporter.

Detective work in finding people with personal reasons for helping can make a big difference. I began this chapter with an example: how Springfield College got me involved. Let me conclude with another example from my own experience, showing how fund raising is helped by the patient, systematic gathering of information.

I received an urgent letter from the late C. E. Peterson, who was then the dean of men at San Diego State. He knew that I had warm memories of my undergraduate days there, and he reminded me that there are always deserving young men and women who need help from scholarship funds. He suggested I might like to donate some money annually for scholarships. To illustrate the need, he enclosed what he called a "typical" letter from an impoverished student who had been helped along the way.

I hadn't given much thought to San Diego State in recent years. In the back of my mind I began phrasing a polite turn-down for Dean Peterson, even as I read the letter he enclosed, which I thought was pretty crude. I glanced through two pages of this hard-sell commercial from the student, wondering if the school actually gave scholarships to such kids, but when I got to the end I knew the Dean had me. The letter was signed "Art Linkletter." I sent a check by return mail, and four students each year since then have been helped by the letter that San Diego State had so carefully kept for two decades.

9 -- FORTUNES AT THE FRONT DOOR

Selling Through Inexperienced Salesmen

An acquaintance of mine has only an eighth-grade education. He isn't what you'd call handsome. In fact, he has a harelip. When he was in the Army his sergeant assigned him to cleaning latrines, just to keep him out of sight. In civilian life he was a consistent loser. By 1967 he had tried twenty-six jobs and failed at all.

Five years later he was selling $200 million worth of cosmetics, clothes, vitamins, wigs, helicopters, and other products in the course of every twelve months. In 1973 the courts put him out of business. His name is Glenn Wesley Turner.

How did this apparently hopeless misfit make his sudden climb to wealth and success, then lose most of what he'd made? He climbed by persuading hundreds of men and women to go and sell house-to-house for him, despite their own lack of experience in salesmanship. They brought in the money for themselves and for him. If he'd limited himself to this kind of operation, he'd still have a flourishing empire today.

As Glenn Turner puts it, "I hope to be remembered as a fellow who created millionaires by making successes out of people nobody would fool with. In my seventy companies you'd find losers, drop-outs, has-beens, and handicapped people of all kinds. There don't have to be any failures in the world. What makes me happy is turning on people to their potential."

A little later I'll tell you more about Turner and his wonder-working sales organization. But first I'd like to point out that neither he nor his salespeople were so very different from other groups that also prosper by peddling products in people's homes.

Turner was just the most dazzling of a long line of successful specialists in "direct selling," as it is called—selling by appointment in the living room or by cold canvass door-to-door.

IGNORANCE BRED SUCCESS

Let me mention a few of Turner's unpromising predecessors in that same long line.

I once read the autobiography of a man who admitted on its second page, "At age twenty I was a country bumpkin, overgrown and awkward. I could scarcely read, could not spell accurately or keep a ledger, and was too shy to impress anyone. . . . I was fired from my first three jobs, after which I went into business for myself. Making and selling brushes was an expedient to which I turned when no one would hire me." This man was Alfred C. Fuller. He founded the Fuller Brush Company and made it a $100-million-a-year business.

More recently in Santa Monica an ex-actor named Tom Hamilton saved enough money to buy the manufacturing rights to Winfield China when the originator, Leslie Winfield Sample, died. Even though 1,800 of America's best department stores stocked this line of dinnerware, and sold about a million dollars worth every year, Tom was dissatisfied. Too many stores simply let Winfield sit on their shelves. They didn't describe its features. They did no selling.

So he literally bet a million dollars that he could do better by taking his cups and saucers to people's front doors. He pulled his line out of retail stores and switched to direct selling. "Competitors said I was committing suicide," he recalls. "Since then I've gone to a few of their funerals." Within five years Tom had 2,000 door-to-door salespeople, and Winfield China sales had quadrupled.

Another good friend of mine is Mrs. Beatrice Birginal of Bensenville, Illinois. In 1945 she and her late husband founded Beeline Fashions, Incorporated, in a back room just nine feet wide. Bee's idea was to persuade her friends to go into their own friends' homes and sell the clothes she designed. Today her company has 20,000 part-time "Beeline Stylists" staging "in-home fashion shows" that sell $80 million worth of clothes a year.

I also know a twenty-seven-year-old southerner named Trine Starnes, who was founder and president of Venus International, Incorporated, a cosmetics company with a big handsome headquarters in Dallas. Trine is the son of a Church of Christ minister. At seventeen he was selling Bibles door to door in Nashville. At eighteen he entered Abilene Christian College but dropped out to try his luck as an insurance salesman. By 1969 he had saved up $1,000 with which he started Venus International. In two years he built an organization of 2,500 Texas men and women selling cosmetics in homes. His company's sales were $224,000 its first year and more than a million dollars its second year. Unfortunately his rate of climb overtaxed his assets and he has been forced out.

Bee Birginal, Tom Hamilton, Alfred Fuller, and Glenn Turner have a great deal in common.

Without any background in business, they became millionaires by applying certain principles that anyone can use.

They learned the art of recruiting hundreds of ordinary people and persuading them to do most of the selling.

This is the art I'll analyze in this chapter. First let's take a look at the background, so we can understand the difficulties.

UNINVITING BUT PROFITABLE

In-home selling, particularly to strangers, is one of the toughest kinds of selling there is. Yet it is a $4 billion-a-year industry which provides profitable employment, full- or part-time, for as many as three million Americans.

About 3,500 companies (including many which have been in business for generations) retail their wares in the home. They make and sell hundreds of things we've come to regard as necessities: cosmetics, toilet articles, food supplements, nursery plants, reducing and exercising equipment, greeting cards, tableware, reference books, vacuum cleaners, and so on.

This whole industry looks unlikely and uninviting when you know its history. Yankee peddlers made many enemies during our pioneer days, when few people could make shopping trips to town. Someone had to take the retail store to them. So hundreds of footloose young fellows shouldered packs and hit the roads to sell beads, buttons, ribbons, patent medicines, razors, scissors, clocks, firearms, and countless other items. If they prospered they might graduate to a packhorse, then to a horse and cart, then to a big four-wheeled shop wagon. If their feet gave out, or a girl caught their fancy, they opened a trading post at a crossroads.

Benedict Arnold was a peddler of coats and caps. Collis P. Huntington, founder of the Southern Pacific Railroad, peddled picks and shovels to prospectors. Isaac Singer, who developed the first practical home sewing machine, sold it himself door to door with a demonstration model on the back of a spring wagon. Adam Gimbel, an immigrant from Bavaria, started as a peddler and went on to found Gimbel's department stores.

Too many of the early cabin-to-cabin peddlers were tricksters. They sold clocks that would run only an hour; hams and cheeses hollowed out and stuffed with sawdust; the famous Connecticut

Glenn W. Turner

nutmeg that was no condiment at all but a wooden replica whittled during dull evenings on the trail. Such sharp practices gradually became so notorious that peddlers had to stay in the far backwoods. But they were long remembered all over America. People of any sophistication never opened their doors to a salesman lest they be tricked.

From Civil War days until about the turn of the century, no respectable sales manager considered for a moment the possibility of a house-to-house campaign. Its chances would be killed by the lingering folklore about peddlers, executives thought.

WHY SOME THINGS SELL AT HOME

But as time passed a few companies began to realize that certain products were naturally adapted to this kind of retail sales. Where a demonstration must be made, the home was the place for it. Experience showed that people at home usually would listen to a complete sales presentation, once the salesman got inside and melted the initial resistance. Those same consumers would watch a demonstration only briefly in stores.

So pedestrian salesmen were tried again. They succeeded in popularizing many new inventions that ordinary retailing had failed to put over: lightning rods, steam cookery aluminum, the sewing machine, the gas stove, the telephone, the carpet sweeper, and the vacuum cleaner.

So we can say that yesteryear's glib salesman with his foot in the door did make some real contributions to the American standard of living. He was followed by lower-pressure people like the Fuller Brush man, the Avon lady, the Real Silk salesman, and Alcoa's Wearever representatives. Ringing millions of doorbells and selling good products all over the country, these sales organizations somewhat softened the hostility that used to confront anyone who tried to sell in the home.

CONSUMERISM VERSUS SALESMEN

Nevertheless, I can't say that the 1970s are the best of times for direct selling. The New Consumerism is the greatest challenge to salesmen in the whole stormy history of salesmanship.

Legislators and bureaucrats, citizens and councilmen, academicians and students, working in more than 500 active consumer organizations, have taken on the character of a mass movement. City and state agencies, prodded by politicians and reformers, race to outdo one another in denouncing and restricting companies that use persuasiveness to move their goods. Class-action lawsuits have cut down such organizations as Glenn Turner's.

Reforms have been needed, of course. We all are consumers and we all need protection from unfair and misleading pressure, as I pointed out in Chapter 3. Thanks mainly to the Federal Trade Commission with its consumer-protection specialists and its advisory boards, deceptions by salesmen aren't as bold as they once were, nor as numerous as you might think.

Door-to-door selling was one of the early targets of the FTC's new Bureau of Consumer Protection. This type of selling is frowned on by some consumer groups. They want to handcuff it if not abolish it altogether.

Actually, selling in the home plays a useful part in the economy. Some of the nation's least tricky companies rely entirely on it—not only those I've already mentioned but other old-timers too, such as Stanley Home Products, Jewel Tea Company, Electrolux, Watkins Products, and dozens of smaller companies that have been in business for more than fifty years. Salesmen for most of these companies simply visit with their customers, display their goods, take orders, deliver, and collect for orders given last time around.

The big objection to direct selling, in the eyes of the New

Consumerism, is the same objection that arose when the first gypsy peddler took to the road: It tempts salesmen into deceit and pressure.

One major deceit is the old ruse of getting into a house by telling the housewife that she has won a special free gift, or by pretending to be taking a poll, or by saying that her minister or her child's teacher suggested the call. The most successful door-to-door salesman of all time, according to legend, was a charming drummer named Percy Beemish who represented Cremo Cosmetics. He used a simple but magical approach. He rang the doorbell, doffed his hat when the lady of the house appeared, and won her with one question: "Girlie, is your mother home?" This was taking unfair advantage of the lady, in the view of consumer protectors.

Another abuse is the trick of talking customers into signing what turns out to be an ironclad contract for years of exorbitant payments. There are recent cases on file of people contracting to pay $264 for goods and services that cost the company only $38.

To block such banditry, the FTC wants a cooling-off rule that would force every salesman to present the housewife with self-addressed forms enabling her to cancel her order within, say, three days. The rule also would include some restrictions on door-opening techniques by making the salesman show his credentials at the door.

Meanwhile the Direct Selling Association, which represents about a hundred leading companies in the field, has actually been lobbying for more federal regulation in the hope that Congress will preempt state and local restrictions on salesmen. At least thirty-three states and ten cities, as I write, have beaten the FTC to the punch by enacting cooling-off and door-closing laws of their own.

These are hard for a regional or national company to live with because they differ so widely. Some regulate only credit sales, others crack down on all cash sales over twenty-five dollars.

Some dictate just what the salesman must say and do in his first few moments with the prospect. To end all this confusion, the Direct Selling Association would prefer one nationwide set of rules drawn up after reasonable debate.

Meanwhile, some companies have clamped down on their own sales crews. One example is Grolier, a big publisher which annually sells about $145 million worth of encyclopedias and reference books. Because of consumer complaints about fast-talking salesmen, Grolier overhauled its door-to-door sales techniques in 1971. Before shipping any order, the company now double-checks with the customer.

Bill Murphy, president of Grolier, says: "We have someone from our credit department—not from our sales department—phone each purchaser and spend about twenty minutes going over the instalment contract to make sure he understands. We want to catch any misstatements by over-eager salesmen. If there's any mix-up which we can't straighten out to the customer's satisfaction, we cancel his order right then, and send back his down payment."

Grolier goes even further. Its headquarters calls a random 10 percent of purchasers two months after they receive the books and asks for their reactions to the books as well as to the salesmen. In addition, the purchasers' contracts entitle them to make collect calls, long distance, to the company if they want to register any complaint.

LET THE SELLER BEWARE

More and more companies are installing toll-free telephone lines for the use of consumers who want to bypass salesmen and dealers and make a complaint directly to headquarters. More than a dozen manufacturers have appointed top-level officers to concentrate solely on consumer affairs. Most companies which sell from the doorstep now insist (as Fuller Brush did from the beginning) that salespeople take a step back when the door is opened and present either company identification or a personal business card. They forbid salesmen to gain entry by pretending to be conducting a survey or by any similar dodge.

We've almost entirely outgrown the ancient rule of Roman common law, "Let the buyer beware." Now the rule is coming to be, "Let the seller beware." He must make sure that his products or services are safe and reliable, that they perform as advertised, and that they are repaired or remedied promptly when they fail. I think every decent company, and its salesmen, are willing to live by this rule.

But I don't say all companies are blameless. A few still give the others a bad name. Recently the New York City Department of Consumer Affairs released a full report, from a salesgirl who had resigned in disgust, of the training she received from one obscure company which sold cheap books for a lot of money. Here's what the company trained her to say at each front door:

"Hi, my name is ————. I'm with Superior Research, and we're speaking to all the mothers in the neighborhood about the Sesame Street album. We've made it part of our child-development program for young children. Do you mind if I ask you a few questions about your opinions on education?"

The salesgirls were then to suggest stepping into the house so they could use a table to write down the answers. After a few sham questions, the girls would go on: "Are you familiar with the work of the Children's Educational Workshop?" (There's no such organization, as far as I know, but the Children's *Television* Workshop produced "Sesame Street.") "Well, how about Project Head Start? As you know, poor people have Head Start to give them an educational advantage, and the rich have private schools, but the middle-class mother felt left out and wanted to have a program that would provide her children with the same opportunities as other children."

The girls would then recite the offerings of the "Workshop"— an information service which, they said, would send two-to twenty-page reports on any question a child asked; pamphlets on child guidance; and the right to purchase "educational materials at half price."

Next the girls were taught to say, "Now, because of the new methods of teaching, we're trying to enroll more mothers in our program. We are currently giving premium inducements for joining the club." The girls would go on to talk about the mothers' club as if they were offering the prospect a chance to join something, not buy something.

The crafty mentor wound up with hints on closing the sale:

> Make up a few names and write them at the top of your enrollment sheet, so it will look like everyone in the neighborhood is joining. Just assume that the mother wants to join, and breeze right into closure. Never ask her to sign anything. Get her signature by telling her "Write down your name for the office," or say "Just okay this application here." Don't tell them that the form is a contract, and don't tell them the total price. If they ask, say that it only costs eighty-nine cents a week. Don't tell them they'll have to pay for 297 weeks. If they object to the price, or seem to hesitate, you should ask, "Aren't you willing to pay eighty-nine cents a week for your child's education?"
>
> After the mother has signed, tell her that our delivery boy will be in the area the next day to bring the books, and ask her whether morning or evening is most convenient. Say that we used to mail the books, but that they were stolen half the time, so now we use our own delivery boys. You gotta make sure the mother will be home when the delivery boy comes, because he's our real salesman. He signs the mother up on a contract to pay about ten dollars a month. He tells her she'll save money by paying at this faster rate.

With even a few such shyster squads ringing doorbells, it's no wonder that some doors are slammed against every in-home salesman.

However, every company in the Direct Selling Association has a liberal refund policy, most of them offer unconditional guarantees, and all are pledged to make sure that "product description be truthful, and terms of sale clearly stated."

Even so, some consumerists want to abolish all direct selling of expensive merchandise. "Just take a look at manuals and training courses for salesmen," they say. "They teach how to greet the prospect agreeably, how to find out what's on her mind, how to ask her opinion, how to lead her into saying something that the salesman can use to his advantage, how to handle objections, and how to ask for the order without seeming to ask for it."

You probably behave this way almost automatically, if you know how to get along with people. Are politeness and a pleasant voice dishonest? Sometimes; many crooks are polite and pleasant. But sometimes I wonder if the consumer movement may contain zealots as well as sensible people. Some of its ferocious activists are selling their ideas with the same high pressure it deplores in commercial salesmen.

Today's consumer movement, which has been gathering steam since the late 1950s, hasn't stopped some people from building big profitable direct-selling organizations. Let's see how they did it.

GOOD WARES DON'T NEED TRICKY SELLING

They started with a product that would almost sell itself.

Then they arranged to peddle this product through part-time salespeople, without much coaching.

To succeed, these people would have to show a housewife a superior product which she needed at a price she could pay. The average woman is a careful buyer, interested in unfamiliar goods, and willing to take time at home to examine them. So the trick would be not to pressure her into buying, but merely to get her to look at what the product would do.

Alfred Fuller found his product in the brushes he made himself. He was no salesman. He got plenty of doors slammed in his face. But he kept ringing doorbells because he faced starvation if he didn't. He found that he had made fifteen sales out of every fifty calls—not through eloquence, but through actions. He washed babies with a back brush, swept stairs, cleaned bottles. When women saw what the brushes would do, they bought them.

Making and selling his brushes might have remained a one-man enterprise if a cousin hadn't awakened him to the possibility of getting other men to go out and sell for him.

Fuller wasn't much of a recruiter. But one of his early salesmen, Frank Beveridge, was. Beveridge spent seventeen years building up Fuller's sales organization, keeping it growing despite constant turnover. Then he left to organize the tremendously successful Stanley Home Products Company, which also sells in the home. Like Fuller, Beveridge found that all he really needed was a line of satisfactory, saleable products.

Many of the star salespeople discovered by Beveridge were "too old, too young, or too unintelligent by the ordinary standards of personnel management," as Fuller recalls. Some were missing an arm or leg or even their eyesight. One successful Fuller Brush man made his rounds in a wheelchair.

So the great truth gradually dawned on Fuller, Beveridge, and others like them: Once you get a good product, you can build sales volume with mediocre salesmen on straight commission. Recruiting hundreds of salespeople, and inducing them to make many calls, is where the persuasiveness comes in.

Glenn W. Turner was spectacularly successful at this. His success came unexpectedly.

In 1967 he was selling sewing machines in the rural South and not doing much better than in twenty-four previous jobs.

Then he happened to hear that several cosmetics companies, encouraged by the great growth of Avon, were experimenting with door-to-door sales. Avon had become the second largest cosmetics house by selling direct to housewives; the direct-sale cosmetics companies' share of the market had tripled in two years. Why shouldn't he jump on their bandwagon?

He gave up the sewing machines, became a distributor for a small cosmetics concern—and wound up broke in a few months.

Maybe the cosmetics weren't very good. Or maybe Glenn hadn't a clue how to sell them. But he had a big idea now, the idea that was to make him rich. He would start his own cosmetics firm and get lots of other people to do the selling.

He started Koscot Interplanetary, Inc.—a company without a product—in a one-room office in Orlando, Florida. Then he wangled a $5,000 loan from a local bank. (This must have been the hardest part of the whole operation. But perhaps he showed the bank that fortunes were being made in cosmetics.) Next he went to New York, found a good commercial laboratory, and contracted with it to produce a line of 104 items: nail polish remover, skin softener, and so on. Mink oil was the base of many of these products.

IT PAYS TO LOOK PROSPEROUS

As his final preparation, Glenn boldly bought a big car and some expensive, flamboyant clothes. This seems to be another common factor in the careers of many persuasive people: cultivating a look of prosperity.

Diamond Jim Brady was a famous case in point. When he got his first job, selling saws to railroads, he bought $200 worth of new clothes and the biggest diamond he could afford. His prospects looked at him and listened. As he made sales he adorned himself with more diamonds, including a 33-carat scarf pin about the size of a locomotive headlight. Sometimes a rough old railroad boss would accuse him of wearing fake jewels—whereupon Brady, beaming, would reach out with one of his diamonds and scratch his name on the office window. Diamonds made him a legend.

A salesman named Al Teetsell was sent from Poughkeepsie to recruit Fuller Brush peddlers in hard-boiled New York City. He made himself noticeable with a diamond ring, ten-dollar neckties, and other finery. From 1923 until his death in 1945, the Fuller Brush salesmen he recruited in New York brought him consistent five-figure earnings.

We might think that flashy clothes would be comic in our sophisticated modern times. But they helped Glenn Turner convince the low-income, half-educated people whom he recruited as his sales force. His flamboyant appearance contrasted with his humble beginnings, which he played up: "You don't think you can sell? Are you a poor farmer's son like me? Are you a grammar-school dropout like me? Do you have a harelip like I do? If I can sell, anybody can! Nobody has to be smart, or good-looking, to succeed in selling. All he needs is confidence!" Looking at Glenn's blinding costume, people decided he was living proof of what he was saying.

GETTING THEIR FEET WET

Then he used another powerful persuasive tool.

He went on, "The worst salesman in the world has at least twenty-five relatives or close friends who'll look at what he has to sell. Start with them. You'll pick up some fat commissions. Then you'll want to go further, and I'll help you."

This was the old, old technique of getting people involved a little at a time, merely asking them to do something easy.

That's how I used to teach frightened kids to swim at the YMCA. I just coaxed them to sit awhile on the side of the pool, dangling their feet and getting used to the feel of the water. Soon they'd be willing to wade. Later I'd get them to splash some water on me and I'd splash back, and so on, little by little, until they were dog-paddling without even thinking about it.

Once I found myself on the receiving end of the same technique. In Brattleboro, Vermont, a master salesman named Cliff Taylor persuaded me to buy skis and take skiing lessons for the first time in my life. I was past fifty, which I thought was too old to learn such a difficult sport. But Cliff was smart. Instead of asking me to try standard skis, which are six feet long and terribly clumsy for a beginner, he showed me a pair of very short learning skis, like big skates. They looked easy. Sure enough, I found I could control them. The taste of success sold me. I've been skiing ever since.

Do you see how Turner used the same psychology in recruiting salespeople? He convinced them that the kind of selling he was talking about would be easy.

All successful direct-selling organizations use this same gentle approach. They've learned that the old-time cold canvass seems too hard—and really is too hard—for amateur salespeople.

Beeline advertises: "We train you to conduct style shows for small informal groups. No investment. No door-to-door. No delivering. No collecting. Phone————for interview."

And when prospects telephone, the Beeline manager concentrates on persuading them to come in for interviews, where she can make her real pitch to sign them up. On the phone she carefully avoids saying anything that would make the job sound hard.

Often a prospect asks, "Is this a selling job?" The manager is trained to respond, "Have you ever done any selling, Mrs. Brown?"

"No I haven't, and I don't want to," the prospect is likely to say. The manager exclaims, "Wonderful, Mrs. Brown! Some of our best stylists have never had any selling experience. Which is better for your interview appointment, 10:00 A.M. on Tuesday or 3:00 P.M. on Wednesday?"

You notice that the manager, like any well-trained persuader, avoids offering the prospect a chance to say No. This is another tested principle. A generation ago Real Silk was training its hosiery salesmen to ask, "How many pair do you want?" rather than, "Would you like to buy some?"

Even the organizations which use only the mail in recruiting their sales force have learned to make the selling job sound easy. The Mason Shoe Company, which has sold in homes since 1904, says in a recruiting letter, "Men and women just like you make a great deal of extra money for themselves just by showing our giant full-color catalog to their friends and neighbors, writing down their orders and sending those orders in to us. . . . You may be telling yourself that these men and women are hot-shot salesmen but if that's what you think, you're wrong! Most of them never sold a thing in their lives before."

At the end of its letter, Mason tries only to get the prospect a little bit involved, rather than hooked all at once:

"The nicest thing about this proposition is that you don't have to go ahead unless you want to. You can send for the catalog, look it over, then decide. Everything is FREE. There's nothing to pay for or return should you decide not to go ahead. Why not mail the postage-free card for your FREE catalog and see for yourself today?"

Thus everything is made inviting. If you do this when you try to persuade, your chances of success are much greater.

By making it sound easy, Avon keeps 400,000 women selling cosmetics. Glenn Turner had 50,000 after only five years in the field. Trine Starnes had 2,500 in Texas alone, after only two years.

SIGNING UP A RELUCTANT ASSISTANT

To digress for a moment, let's consider a slightly different problem in one-man recruitment. It was solved with the same gentle getting-the-feet-wet technique.

Whitelaw Reid, managing editor of the New York *Herald Tribune,* had spotted a brilliant young writer named John Hay and wanted him to take a job on the staff. But Hay, a former assistant private secretary to President Lincoln, was homeward bound to Illinois to practice law. How could Reid get him to change all his plans?

Instead of making a blunt offer, Reid took the young man to dinner. He said nothing about a job. After dinner he proposed a stroll over to the *Tribune* office. There he found (as usual) that some important news had come in by telegraph. He said to Hay, "I'm short-handed tonight. Could you sit down and write this story? It won't take long."

Hay could hardly refuse. The task was easy and interesting. He liked the bustling atmosphere of the newsroom. Then Reid asked him to fill in for an absent editor "just for a week." Hay stayed on for five years as editor and writer, helping to make Whitelaw Reid famous and enabling him to succeed Horace Greeley as owner and publisher of the most powerful newspaper of that era.

When we tempt people to do something that will be easy for them, yet which is worth doing and which opens their way to additional benefits, we give them an almost irresistible incentive.

Similar strategy works well in the actual process of selling merchandise. On the proven principle that "tryers are buyers," the direct-selling organizations show their salespeople how to get potential customers involved. For example, Fuller puts a brush in the prospect's hand so she tries it for herself. Vacuum cleaner salesmen don't just demonstrate, they ask the housewife to participate in the demonstration. American Ceramics has a more spectacular stunt: It invites the housewife to hammer nails with a china cup, or to stand on a dinner plate, so she convinces herself of the strength of the chinaware.

A good cosmetics salesman doesn't say a word as he begins his sales routine. He just put a bottle of lotion in the hands of the housewife. What's easier than for her to take it and look at it? Then he opens his demonstrator bottle and pours some lotion on her hand as he takes back the bottle she has been holding. Automatically she rubs the lotion into her hands as he croons, "Notice how refreshing this lotion is. Feel how your skin drinks it in. See how quickly it's absorbed? Doesn't it have a delightful aroma? Notice how soft your skin begins to feel already. Once you've tried this new lotion you'll never be without it." He has enlisted sight, touch, smell, and hearing. No wonder cosmetics sell well in homes.

NOT AS A STRANGER

As I remarked earlier, a total stranger has a tough time selling in homes. That's why direct-selling organizations nowadays don't send their people into homes as strangers. They ease them in as friends already known to the prospects, visiting by appointment.

Glenn Turner always had his recruits start by approaching their own friends and relatives. As the next step, he coached these recruits to ask for introductions to other neighbors and friends. His Koscot salespeople said, "If you'll see to it that I just get in to talk, whether I sell or not, you get a fifty-dollar supply of Koscot goods."

Other companies do the same. It's known to the trade as club plan selling, and it's particularly useful in selling big-ticket items such as carpets, silverware, and chinaware. Under the plan every customer receives additional merchandise free or at discounts for each friend she gets to join the club. (People join by buying merchandise.) Each new member can win similar bonuses for getting her friends to join, and so on ad infinitum. Thus nobody need try to sell strangers.

Another approach is the "party plan" of selling through "style shows," as Beeline calls them, or "beauty shows," in the phrase of some cosmetics companies, or Stanley Home Products' "home parties."

Under such a plan, a hostess invites a group of her friends in for the demonstration. She serves refreshments, and receives a merchandise prize for giving the party (plus other prizes, usually, for the number of guests who agree to give similar parties.) Guests are told in advance, "Leave your money at home," so everyone is relaxed and natural. The company's part-time representative (called stylist or beauty adviser or anything that doesn't suggest that alarming word "selling") often says, "Look, I'm not a salesman. I'm just a housewife like you. I've tried these products myself and I can answer questions about them, but I won't try to sell you."

Then the guests can "shop" in a congenial atmosphere with no feeling of pressure, obligation, or commercialism. They also get more personal attention from the saleslady than they're likely to get in an average retail store. Occasionally some guest will speak up in praise of a product or will mention new ways she has found to use it. If it's a "fashion show," the guests cluster around the sample rack and begin trying on the clothes. The saleslady fills in the order form.

If a sales representative is energetic about lining up hostesses, she can hold two or three such parties every week and will probably makes sales to most of the guests. It's far better than pounding pavements.

Party-plan selling is profitable because the parties perpetuate themselves. Several guests at each party are generally glad to serve as hostesses for future parties, so the potential keeps multiplying. Sales through the party plan are reported to total more than $200 million a year. Stanley Home Products alone has booked as many as 12,000 parties for a single day, and it averages sales of forty dollars to fifty dollars per party.

ASK FOR REFERRALS

I think there's a lesson here for all salesmen: Use one customer to get new ones. The best prospect tips come from satisfied customers.

Beeline reminds its 20,000 sales representatives with every mailing: "Being a successful stylist amounts to only one thing: bookings! Think bookings! Expect bookings! Always join the guests for refreshments, and discuss booking dates with those you have not previously approached."

Elmer Leterman, one of the greatest insurance salesmen, expands the same principle into this thought: "Every client of yours works somewhere. In most cases he works alongside other people. So you have a nest of prospects. Nurses in a hospital, teachers in a school, stenographers in an office building, workers in a factory are examples. Finding prospects must be continuous!"

Another famous salesman, Frank Bettger, phrases the same advice vividly: "Never let a sale run into a dead end. Always play position for the next shot."

Here's how one hardware salesman uses current customers. He says, "Mr. Jones, over in Anaheim there's a store which is almost exactly like yours. I've never been able to sell them a dollar's worth. I wonder if you'd mind dictating a little note to them outlining your experience with us and the success you've had in selling our goods." He makes it a point to have the old customer in one town and the prospect in another, since he certainly wouldn't ask for help in selling to the dealer's own competitors.

THE PERILS OF PYRAMIDING

Glenn Turner apparently pushed the referral principle too far. He started selling Koscot distributorships at $5,000, and paid these distributors $3,000 for each new distributor they brought in. Nobody had an exclusive territory. But almost everybody figured he could earn more by selling Koscot distributorships than by selling Koscot products.

Meanwhile he also started selling Dare To Be Great courses in salesmanship and self-motivation. The course came in four steps. People who spent $2,000 to buy the first three steps earned the right to sell the course to others for a $900 commission. Purchasing the fourth step for another $5,000 entitled the buyer to sell Dare To Be Great courses at a $2,000 commission.

It was like a chain letter system. Everyone paid Turner and expected to recoup by pyramiding. Turner soon found himself under legal fire in forty states and from the Federal Trade Commission.

He first came to trial in Florida, where he was charged with violating state laws by selling "unregistered securities"—i.e., the rights to sell Dare To Be Great courses. Hundreds of his supporters cheered him outside the courtroom, and the jury hopelessly deadlocked on whether his course franchises were really securities.

No court ever did find fault with the products or services sold through Turner's companies. However, many unhappy people who had bought distributorships in hopes of earning huge incomes brought class-action suits against him. A number of these were consolidated in one federal court. After months of hearings, Turner agreed to a settlement that liquidated Glenn W. Turner Enterprises Inc. and distributed $4,700,000 in assets among his distributors. One of the attorneys who brought suit told a reporter, "A great many people will exclude them-selves from the settlement because they idolize Turner."

Undoubtedly a lot of people were sorry to see him go out of business. Some of the lawmen had bought Koscot cosmetics for their wives and reordered later. Turner had given $2,500,000 to charity, including a million dollars to build an opportunity center for retarded children in his native South Carolina. He was Florida's largest employer of the handicapped.

It was perfectly logical for him to hire the handicapped, just as Fuller Brush and Stanley Home Products have been doing for decades. The direct-selling field is almost the only one that puts up no discriminatory barriers. Age, sex, physical handicaps, lack of education, lack of money, or other disadvantages are irrelevant in selling. Great-grandmothers and teenagers have equal chances for success.

Fred Grair of Cleveland, a Negro who was a bootblack in 1947, has averaged more than $15,000 annually for the last quarter-century while selling Kirby vacuum cleaners. Some Beeline salespeople are averaging $30,000 and $40,000 a year in commissions. Many of these are women; sometimes their husbands retire or go into partnership with them.

But this isn't to say that the average person gets rich through in-home selling. McKinsey & Company, management consultants, once made an intensive study which found that average annual earnings for direct salesmen varied from a low of $92 in one company to a high of $700 in another, even though their commissions ranged around 30 percent or more. This means that most companies have a few people making good-to-bountiful sales and earnings and many people making tiny sales and earnings.

The fact is that relatively few people make sizable incomes at this type of work. Turnover among salespeople may be 70 percent to 90 percent a year. Countless recruits who might succeed with proper training quit before ever tasting success. There are rude rebuffs in any kind of sales work, and this is too hard on the ego of the average person.

Part-time salespeople—like most human beings—tend to be lazy. As Pamela Bowlin wrote, "Most of us live our lives the way we watch television. Even though the program isn't as good as we'd like it to be, we're too lazy to get up and change it."

Consequently, a company which simply left salespeople on their own wouldn't last long in the direct-selling field. Successful companies have a rip-roaring local sales meeting every week or at least monthly. Morale-building is a major enterprise.

There are banners and slogans on the walls. There are fight songs. The meeting chairman may announce in elated astonishment that no fewer than five men have done so well in the last month that they've won big prizes for themselves and their wives. (*Cheers.*) Tell us, says the chairman, how you did it. (*Yay, tell us!*)

The testimonials are like those at old-time revival meetings. One man reminds his brethren that "When it's raining out there, housewives are waiting for us in every home." (*Cheers and whistles.*) Another tells them the only reason for not making $600 a week is not working. (*Clapping and cheering.*) Then up rises the district manager with the final exhortation. "Let's give credit to our product. It's the best. You are the greatest selling organization in America." (*YEEOW! Yessir! Amen!*) "For everyone who sells six this week, I'll throw a champagne steak brunch, and those who sell seven get a free weekend with your wife, everything paid including transportation, at the company's guest ranch."

A leading company like Scott & Fetzer, which sells Kirby vacuum cleaners in the home, spends around $900,000 a year on pepping up its salesmen. One year it gave Cadillacs to twenty-one distributors in a contest based on quota sales. Another year fifteen Continentals were awarded. Every year about a hundred contest-winning salesmen are flown to Cleveland with their wives to be partied and exhorted. The wives are invited to a style show where they pick out any $250 outfit they want. Each year about 175 cash prizes, totaling $50,000, go to fifty-odd winners of Kirby sales contests.

Even a quiet, rural, low-pressure company like Mason Shoe, which I believe works on its salesmen entirely through the mail, keeps them selling with offers like "Get free shoes for life when you take as few as five orders a month for Mason shoes!"

A more noisy outfit such as Venus held a statewide meeting every month, awarded Cadillacs to top salespeople and top recruiters, announced new contests frequently, and once or twice a year took more than a hundred "qualifiers for the President's Club" to a glamorous spot like Acapulco for an all-expenses-paid vacation.

At Glenn Turner's meetings he would introduce someone like a blind ex-Marine who was pitting olives in a pizza parlor at forty-eight dollars a week until he began selling the Koscot line and making $30,000 a year. Or Glenn might bellow to the crowd, "What I'm selling is attitude! I'm showing people how they can make something of themselves! If you give a man a fish, you feed him for one day, but if you show him how to fish, you feed him for life. That's what I do! I found some products that are easy to sell because they're darn good. They made me a millionaire in five years. I'm not the only one. I want you to listen to this lady who earned $25,000 in sales commissions last year. Look at her! Withered arm. Paralyzed leg. They're no handicaps in selling our line. Tell 'em how to do it, Emma!"

Emma said something like this: "I found out that when I sat down with people and just told them the truth about these products, quite a few people bought. All I do is show them to my friends. There's no high pressure, no smooth talk. Just

keep everlastingly busy, making appointments to see folks.
That's the big secret. Why don't you get your friends to help
you? For every friend you recruit to sell Koscot, you get a percentage of what they sell. That's what I did. I used to be too
shy to talk to anybody. But I finally tried—and found out it
was easy. If I can do it, all you folks can too."

There is a firm truth beneath all this hurrah and razzmatazz.
It's an age-old promise from the Bible: "All things are possible
to him who believeth." And it's backed up by a factual report
from the leading psychologist of his time, William James:
"The greatest discovery of my generation is this: We have
learned that we can alter our lives by altering our attitudes of
mind."

One of the highest challenges in the whole art of persuasion
is persuading people to feel confident. It's the problem of every
sales manager, every athletic coach, every theatrical director,
every business leader, every religious leader, and social worker.
Glenn Turner met the challenge with large numbers of run-
of-the-mill people. The other direct-selling leaders use much
the same methods—

Make it easy to start.

Offer tempting inducements.

Show convincing proofs that others are succeeding.

When these organizers add a little know-how and show-how,
they often make their pupils rich. I think their methods are
worth studying.

10 -- SO YOU'RE THE SALES MANAGER

Spurring Salesmen to Success

"Our chief want in life is somebody who shall make us do what we can," according to Ralph Waldo Emerson. Of all the pithy and profound remarks by this New England sage, few pack more insight into a single sentence.

Somebody who shall make us do what we can: Every human being needs him and probably we salesmen need him more than most. He may multiply our sales if he gets us to do our best. We are just as human, just as prone to weaknesses and faults as our customers. Every now and then we get lazy. Or we get blue. Or we see red. Or we slip into a rut. Or we lose our nerve.

Selling isn't easy. It takes enthusiasm, and enthusiasm often needs pumping up by "somebody who shall make us do what we can."

How does a successful sales manager help his salesmen succeed?

Not by fear primarily. Threats to fire a salesman, or to penalize him in other ways, usually tear down his ego and tempt him to seek another job (or maybe to sabotage the sales manager if he can).

Nor does a sales manager get the best from his men primarily by giving them perfect advice and instructions. True, part of his job is to figure out plans and to communicate those plans—to advise salesmen where and when to make their calls, what to say, how to say it. Whole books have been written on the scientific side of sales management—on selection of salesmen, on incentive plans, on quotas and targets, on study of customers' changing needs, on selection of products to push, and so on. But after the plans are made, the salesmen must be sold on executing them. Here is where science ends and art begins.

NO PERSUASION? NO ACTION

Once when President Kennedy was asked what surprised him most as President, he confessed, "I had no idea it would be so difficult to get programs put into action." This same unpleasant surprise has dismayed generations of teachers, publicists, executives, and statesmen. They thought that if they pointed out the right course their audience would follow it automatically.

One famous case history in planning and persuasion is the story of the U.S. agricultural extension service, pioneered early in this century by the Department of Agriculture. This ambitious program was planned to achieve big gains in crop yields by teaching farmers to use the expert farming techniques worked out in agricultural colleges and experimental stations.

The techniques would put money in the farmers' pockets and save them hours of hard toil. You might think (if you hadn't learned otherwise through your own experiences in selling) that farmers would eagerly accept the new methods. But of course they didn't.

Writing in the *Harvard Business Review*, Raymond W. Miller described "long and disillusioning experience with bulletins, the lecture platform, the farmers' institute, government farms, exhibition trains, and so on . . . all of which, it was sadly learned, accomplished very little."

Finally the Department realized what was needed: constant face-to-face persuasion. It sent men called county agents to call on farmers regularly and win them over to the new methods. It was county agents who sold the farmers on the Department's program, thereby doubling America's crops of cotton, corn, and many other staples.

Any plan must be sold to the people who will carry it out, whether they are farmers working for themselves, buyers looking for bargains, or salesmen on a payroll. Paradoxically, the paid employee is usually the hardest to convert to a better method.

Chester I. Barnard, formerly president of the New Jersey Bell Telephone Company, made a study of this problem and pointed out that an employee will act on instructions only if four conditions are fulfilled: (1) he must understand the instructions; (2) he must be mentally and physically able to comply; (3) he must be convinced that the instructions are consistent with the company's purpose; and (4) he must be convinced that the instructions are also compatible with his personal interests, i.e., that he has something to gain by following the instructions, or at least has nothing to lose.

This highlights the urgent need for persuasiveness, for salesmanship, in managing any crew of salesmen. The salesmen will do as they please unless their manager fulfills the four conditions listed above.

Therefore, the manager must first make sure his men understand the instructions. (He can do this best through the give-and-take of face-to-face conversation, just as a salesman watches a prospect's reactions and asks leading questions whenever this seems advisable.) Beyond this the manager must convince, persuade, and inspire his men to make full use of their own talents.

PERSUADERS ON THE PLAYING FIELDS

Let's look at some masters of the art of "making people do what they can," to adapt Emerson's phrase.

Astute athletic coaches learn this art, and sales managers can profit by imitating the best of them. Isn't a sales manager a coach? Don't salesmen and athletes have a great deal in common? They need perseverance, fortitude, and faith in themselves.

"The important thing is not to panic. You have to grind, day after day, and forget about yesterday," said a great baseball manager, Fred Hutchinson, who took over the seventh-place St. Louis Cardinals and guided them to the top of the National League, although they'd been 10-1 outsiders in preseason betting. "I try to make a ballplayer believe in himself. We haven't got the best club, but they believe in themselves. They go out every day and grind. Baseball doesn't have many naturals, a lot less than you might imagine. The ones who work hardest are the ones who make it, the ones who win. Sometimes that's the only difference. If you don't work hard at this game, you might as well hang them up. Sweat is your only salvation."

He might have been talking about salesmen.

Until his tragic death from cancer, Fred kept his Cardinals believing in themselves and staying near the top. How? Through sheer force of personality, in the opinion of the Cardinal general manager, Frank Lane. "I knew we were going to have to build with young players, and I needed a manager who could handle them. Fred had a rough, tough demeanor, but he had that damnable patience. I even accused him of being a character-builder. I think he was unimaginative as a strategist, but he went right on getting results."

Bob Broeg, St. Louis *Post-Dispatch* sportswriter, summed up Fred in part when he wrote: "He is a man who has a way

Coach Dean B. Cromwell

with men. . . . He makes no pretense of maneuvering or manipulating. If, as a tactician, Hutchinson is uninspired, he has the right quality of holding the confidence and loyalty of his players. The Cardinals like their rugged manager. He has them believing they can win."

Hutchinson was famous throughout baseball for his monumental rage to win. The frustration of losing a close game could ignite a temper in which he smashed water coolers, stools, and light bulbs. Once in Cincinnati he punched a wall until his knuckles were swo'ı ı and bloody. But—and this was the key to his success—his rages were almost never directed at individual players. Knowing his own ferocity, Fred made himself wait overnight before criticizing a player for a mistake.

Sarcasm, the sharp weapon of many baseball managers, was no part of Fred's nature. This man of short temper had an amazing reservoir of patience with young players and a deep compassion for ballplayers in general. Perhaps this was because of his own experience. He had been a pitcher, but he'd never possessed great natural ability. So he knew how difficult the game could be.

If you are aiming for the top as a sales manager, maybe you can learn from Fred Hutchinson: Be patient with your salesmen. Remember how difficult their work is. Keep them believing in themselves so that they'll go out every day and grind.

MORALE MAKES THE DIFFERENCE

When morale is high, almost any style of operation will succeed, even the slave-driving style. The U.S. Marine Corps, famous for both its discipline and its morale, succeeds partly because (1) its rigorous training gives men confidence in themselves, and (2) every Marine officer is taught that he exists only to increase the effectiveness of the enlisted men. Officers and men trust each other.

Eddie Erdelatz, the Naval Academy's football coach during the 1950s, was not a notably hard-driving type, yet he turned out teams that beat bigger and heavier Army teams year after year. When he first took over, famous pro coach Red Strader said, "If anybody can restore Navy's morale, it's Erdelatz. He's a terrific salesman and will sell himself to his players. They'll swear by him—and that's a coaching gift."

After Eddie's teams had upset Army four times, a reporter asked a veteran squad member what the secret was. The answer: "Eddie never let us get discouraged. No matter how many times we lost, he left us believing we could win."

On the other hand, Vince Lombardi, who made the Green Bay Packers perennial champions of pro football, was a savage taskmaster. He berated, threatened, swore, levied big fines, even kicked and slapped his players. He got away with it (where most martinets fail sooner or later) because the men loved him despite his Simon Legree ways. They knew he was dedicated to their success. And he knew when to give the slap on the back that put new life in them.

In *Instant Replay,** Jerry Kramer's vivid book about life with Lombardi, he tells of sitting exhausted and aching after hours of practice, wondering whether he should quit, when he felt Vince's hand rumpling his hair. "Jerry," the coach said, "one of these days you're going to be the greatest guard in the league." That was all it took. Jerry was ready to go back out to practice for another four hours.

Enlightened coaches know how important psychology is. Ara Parseghian, with a long record of success at Northwestern and Notre Dame, has said: "Strategy is very important, I'll grant you. But the ability to put this thing together moralewise is more important than anything else. It's the personnel, the people who do the job and how they feel about doing their job. If you could control this one factor, you'd be amazed at the things you could do."

* World Publishing Company, New York, N.Y., 1968.

I was often fascinated to watch one of the greatest of all masters at getting people to believe in themselves: Dean Cromwell, track coach at University of Southern California. In his thirty-nine-year career at USC his teams won twenty-one national championships; he produced thirteen world record holders plus three relay teams that set world records; in all Olympic Games from 1912 until his retirement in 1949, at least one of his athletes won a gold medal. Something like forty Trojans became individual national champions under his guidance. What other coach has ever approached such a record?

In getting phenomenal performance from his athletes, Dean used quite a repertoire of psychological principles. Let's see what he did that can be valuable to you as a sales manager, or even as a salesman, in certain situations.

A CHAMPION-MAKER IN ACTION

To begin with, Dean was a great believer in keeping everyone in an optimistic mood, a happy, enthusiastic mood. He didn't give fiery pep talks. He may have read Gilbert Highet's essay on "The Art of Persuasion,"* which pointed out:

> Persuasion must work on the emotions as well as on the mind. Human beings were suffering fear and anger, enjoying hope and pleasure, long before they were able to think clearly. Their emotions still lie deeper than their reason, sometimes work against their reason, and should always be harmonized with their reason. Persuasion will be most effective when it begins with the emotions. Therefore we ought to start persuading—before introducing any arguments—by calming and smoothing, pleasing and flattering. Surgery never begins until the patient is anesthetized. Persuasion should never start until the patient has been made receptive.

* *The Arts of Living*, New York, N.Y., Simon & Schuster, 1954.

Dean made people receptive by his manner. He was a genial, talkative extrovert, always laughing, joking, flattering, or kidding. But he once told me—and I think it was extremely important: "I always kid on the upside, never the downside. I never make fun of anyone."

Never a putdown, always a buildup. He hailed all his athletes, "Hi, Champ!" He called the ladies Bright Eyes or Goldilocks. Even his casual acquaintances were "my handsome friend" or "my well-dressed friend."

Do you see the magic in this? It's amazing how you brighten the atmosphere just by smiling at people, "jollying" them along, flattering them outrageously and amusingly. Everyone enjoys a compliment, especially a joking compliment that calls for no response. Deep down, people half-believe even the most grandiloquent praise. Subconsciously their self-esteem is fortified. So they're in a receptive mood for whatever comes next.

Dean went farther than greeting each athlete as Champ. He would introduce an athlete of less than record-breaking calibre to a stranger with: "I want you to meet the fastest miler in the U.S.A." or, "Let me present one of the fastest sprinters in captivity" or, "This is the future Olympic champion shot-putter." Even a stray salesman would hear himself introduced by Dean as "the genial and charming salesman for the Wilson Sporting Goods Company."

In addition, Dean made a point of climaxing the introduction with the person's full name. He called the man who was his first and most publicized champion "Charles William Paddock," instead of "Charlie Paddock" or just plain Charlie. His ace weight thrower, Bud Houser, later became a dentist, and always thereafter in mentioning him, Dean rumbled out a resounding "Dr. Lemuel Clarence (Bud) Houser." Rival athletes on other teams were referred to, even in their absence, as "the great Owens" or "the great Hartranft."

Of course all this flowery rhetoric was slightly ridiculous, which made it fun. Dean believed in lightening up the monot-

onous grind of training with a good-humored flow of talk.
Whenever a boy topped his own best mark, Dean would remind him exuberantly, "That's a new world's record, for you!
Keep on improving, and you'll make me look like a great
coach!"

The value of humor, of setting a light-hearted mood, is so
important that I'd like to expand it further, even at the cost
of digressing from Dean Cromwell, to whom we'll return in a
moment.

LAUGHING LEADERS

Most successful leaders in every line of endeavor try to in-
ject humor here and there, for many purposes. For one thing,
it keeps their listeners alive and attentive because they're never
quite sure what is coming next. For another, as we've seen, a
laugh lightens what otherwise could be a depressing atmosphere. For example, there was one terribly tense situation during World War II in Burma, when the British Field Marshal,
Viscount William J. Slim, needed a way to reassure his staff
after a major defeat. "Things could be worse," he began.

"How?" asked a voice from the rear.

"Well," said Slim, "it could be raining."

Similarly, General (and later President) Eisenhower had a
way of putting people at ease with a joke. His door was always open to members of his staff, and whenever he spied
some subordinate pausing timidly on the threshold of his office, he would flash a grin and shout, "Come in, dammit. Don't
act as if this were a boudoir."

Pete Daland, who has coached USC swimmers to a long
string of national championships, is a hard driver but a hu-
morous one. If swimmers moan about strong chlorine in the

water, Pete may reply that the chlorine is really a blessing because it keeps them from noticing the smoggy Los Angeles air. To a group of drooping athletes, standing dejected after a grueling practice series, he has bellowed: "Hold up your heads, you guys. Breathe in that good fresh air coming through the windows. Who opened those windows for you? Your coach did. Your coach did this for you because he is always loyal to his team!"

Pete is a brisker and tauter type than Cromwell, but he has adopted a Cromwellian manner of building up athletes with fancy introductions to visitors. He may present one of his boys as "This is Brian Foss, 17:26 at Bartlesville last year." Or after introducing a national champion like Roy Saari, he might continue, "Roy Saari is an easy-moving, semi-reptilian animal who is constantly dangerous." Pete often introduced big John Konrads as "the bear that swims like a man."

THE RIGHT KIND OF BRAGGING

Notice another technique that Daland and Cromwell had in common: They habitually bragged about an athlete in his presence. In fact, on the practice field Dean would bawl, "Look what he did!" loud enough to attract the whole squad, whenever a man topped his own best mark.

You might think that such glad-handing would give the recipient a swelled head, but it didn't because Pete and Dean combined it with constant exhortations to try harder. Athletes (and salesmen) *will* try harder when they are subconsciously seeking to live up to a handsome self-image. Anyone will.

Did a friend ever say to you, "You're very thorough," or "You're amazingly punctual"? You still remember it, don't you? Even small compliments stick in our minds, and we automatically shape ourselves to fit them. Thus you can be 95 percent sure that if Bill Jones has been adequately conscientious and he hears you tell people, "Our man William Henry Jones is a fantastically dedicated salesman," he won't make a liar out of you. As for the 5 percent who merely puff up under such treatment, they're inflated anyway and life will deflate them. You're interested in the others, the normal human beings, who get fired up for further effort when they feel the warm glow that comes from spoken recognition of their worth.

Some sales managers carry this principle a step further. They ask a successful salesman to write (or to give orally) an explanation of what he does and how he does it. Such explanations can stimulate other salesmen; over and over the manager tells them, "This is how our successful salesmen do it," quoting the names of the crack salesmen.

THE POWER OF COMPARING PEOPLE

Shakespeare said that comparisons are odious. They needn't be. They can be stimulating if you use them as Dean Cromwell did. One year he had a champion pole-vaulter named Bill Sefton. He also had an unproven sophomore vaulter, Earle Meadows. Every time Sefton improved his own mark, the jolly Dean would tell Meadows, "You can do it if Bill can." The day came when Sefton broke the world's record. A few minutes later Meadows tore down the runway and tied it.

You might think such a double triumph could happen only once in a century. Wrong. Whenever Phil Cope scampered over the hurdles in 14.6 seconds, Dean told Roy Staley, "If Phil can do it, you can. You've got everything he's got." Finally Cope and Staley ran a dead heat in 14.2 seconds. When they did, it was the world's record for the event. Dean got comparable results many times. He knew that two of the most potent words in the dictionary are "You can."

A feat sometimes looks impossible to someone. Then he is

shown that someone like himself did it. He promptly does it too. All he needed was to be convinced that it was within his power. Comparisons are a great tonic if they're upbeat. Never ask a man, "Why can't you sell as much as Jones?" Tell him buoyantly, "If Jones sells that much, you will too! You're as good as he is!"

And when someone fails? Remind him of others who failed worse and came back to succeed.

For example, you might mention Abraham Lincoln. Voters rejected him in six lesser elections before they elected him President. Another such example is a man who failed as a soldier, a farmer, and a real estate agent, and at age thirty-eight sank into a humble job as bookkeeper and wagon-driver for a leather merchant. Who could have predicted that within eight years this discredited handyman, Ulysses Grant, would lead a million soldiers to victory and then win the Presidency?

For more current examples, you might mention a college dropout named Edwin H. Land, who failed to sell his Polaroid process to camera companies, but didn't quit trying and eventually became a multimillionaire. Or Chester F. Carlson, who was turned down by every major manufacturer of office equipment the first time he tried to sell them his new process of photocopying called Xerox.

UPLIFTING THE DOWNCAST

There's more we can learn from Dean Cromwell. I've heard countless tales about Trojan tracksters who were tired, discouraged, or off form on the day of a meet, yet performed superbly when this coach used his psychology on them. He never lied to them; they would have seen through false bombast at once. He simply used facts to convince them of their own powers.

Here's one true tale about Dean. In the middle of a big

meet he noticed that his ace distance runner, Louis Zamperini, looked downcast.

"Anything wrong, Champ?" Dean asked.

"I can't run a good race on this track," he muttered. "It's too hard. It's dead. It hurts my legs."

Instead of barking at him for his defeatist mood, Dean roared with laughter. "The best you could do out there in the two-mile race was 9:12—pathetic, wasn't it, Champ? Twice as far as you have to run this time! Only 9:12 and you were grinning when you hit the finish line." The grin was back on Zamperini's face as he walked onto the track for the mile race. He won.

Zamperini, like everyone else, didn't realize his own capabilities. If you keep telling people they can outdo themselves, they will. According to Dean, this was the whole foundation of his success in coaching.

Here's a more elaborate example of Dean's marvelous gift of salesmanship. One year in the Pacific Coast championship meet his team came down to the last event, the mile relay, only five points ahead of Stanford. This was bad, because Stanford's relay team had recently set a world record and was a certain winner. If the Trojans could get at least the single point for fifth place in the race they would win the meet. But the trouble was that Cromwell hadn't planned to enter the relay, because he had only one fast quarter-miler. Four other colleges were entering powerful relay teams. Even if the Trojans entered, they seemed sure to finish sixth and last.

PERSUADING FOUR PESSIMISTS

Dean gathered four of his glum runners and went to work on them. Beaming with confidence, he told Zamperini (who had run himself out in winning the mile, and hadn't been able to finish the half-mile): "Louie, you'll lead off. A nice little lap around the track will get that tension out of your legs and send you home feeling like a million. Just follow the boys around and take it easy. Don't run hard unless you feel like it at the finish."

Then he turned to Art Laret, a low hurdler who was out of breath because his race had just ended. "Laret, you finished that race looking as fresh as a daisy! Anyone who can step over the sticks like you will find striding this flat race just a breeze. So you run our second lap."

For the third lap he chose Art Reading, a half-miler who was deeply doleful after finishing fifth in his own event. "Reading, the way you sprinted up from nowhere to score a point in that half-mile shows you're full of speed today. Put the same kick at the end of your relay lap and you'll start Howard out where he can pick someone off."

Dean gazed proudly at Howard Upton, the lone quarter-miler, who likewise had disappointed himself with a fifth-place finish in his own race. "Upton, you're the best 440 man in this meet. It wasn't your fault you got elbowed and pocketed in the race today. Now go out and show 'em how a champ can run without interference!"

When the relay started, a relaxed Zamperini ran a faster quarter-mile than he'd ever run when fresh. Laret also equalled his best practice time for the distance. However, the rest of the field had gone far ahead, and Reading was twenty yards behind the nearest man when he entered the far turn. Then he came to life with a finishing sprint, just as Dean had predicted he could, and was only eight yards behind when he passed the baton. It was the fastest 440 of his life. Upton ran one of his best races and passed not one man but two, giving Troy fourth place and a two-point margin in the meet.

This was typical of Dean's salesmanship. He picked out men's good points and kept talking about them. When they did poorly, he gave them reasons why they were likely to improve.

"This practice track is slow, so you'll surely be faster on the stadium track," Dean might say. "The wind has bothered you, so running will seem easier inside the stadium walls, won't it? . . . You haven't felt well, so you're bound to improve as soon as you've rested enough to get in top shape."

Dean worked hardest on the weaker competitors. (As did Vince Lombardi, incidentally. Most of his compliments went to rookies.) Dean's favorite psychology on a runner was to put him through a time trial, at top speed, of three-fourths the runner's usual distance. As soon as the man finished, Cromwell was walking beside him. "Look, Champ," he would say excitedly, showing his stopwatch. "You did three fine quarters: 62, 63, 62. And look at you! You've almost stopped panting already. Feel your legs—they're loose and limber. Now, here's what we'll do in the race. We'll slow you down by two seconds in each of those first three laps. That will leave you so fresh you can do the last lap in 60. You've run it that fast many times. So you'll make your mile in 4:13. We know the man you'll race can't break 4:15. So just take it easy until the race, and we'll get that guy!" Maybe the Trojan miler had never broken 4:15 either, but Dean's facts were valid, and Dean's conviction was so genuine that the runner was convinced too. More likely than not, he ran his race in 4:12.

Optimism must be convincing to be helpful. So in using Dean's technique, do what Dean did: Aim for a reasonable goal. If a salesman sold nine boxes yesterday, show him why he can sell ten or twelve today.

As in all selling, enthusiasm and friendliness count for a lot. To quote Emerson again, "Nothing great was ever accomplished without enthusiasm. Keep enthusiastically excited about what you are doing." If the people you manage see your enthusiasm, that you're genuinely interested in their success, that you're ready to help the slow and correct the confused in a friendly way, they'll be receptive to whatever you tell them. They will reflect back your enthusiasm.

DIRECTORS ARE SALESMEN, TOO

Joshua Logan's enthusiasm made him one of Broadway's greatest directors. He often brought out the best in people because he positively crackled with excitement about their projects, with desire to help them succeed, with gusto, appreciation, and energy.

Josh took as much interest in other directors' plays as in his own. "This is going to be the God-damnedest show ever!" he would roar. "It's going to win the Pulitzer Prize!" And more than once, by the time Josh finished helping, the play actually did win a Pulitzer.

Elia Kazan (another ace director) once recalled, "You'll be on the road, beating your brains out and wondering what to do next, when all of a sudden you'll look up the aisle and there comes Josh. One night while I was out of town directing a play, I was really bushed after the performance. All I wanted to do was sleep. Along came Josh. He insisted we talk about the show. He kept me up till dawn, giving me advice. He got so worked up that he began to make me feel I wasn't sufficiently interested in my own play."

When Josh directed a cast, his explanation of how he wanted a line interpreted was far more dramatic than the line itself. In a rehearsal of *Mister Roberts*—toward the climax of the scene in which the ship's doctor manufactured Scotch whiskey out of medical alcohol, hair tonic, and other ingredients—the doctor's line was, "We're on the right track!" Josh thought the actor spoke the line with insufficient verve.

"No, no!" Josh shouted, charging down the aisle and instantly becoming the doctor himself. "Like *this!* We're on the right track, by God! We'll get the son of a bitch! We'll get those bastards yet! When we get 'em, we'll *kill* 'em! That way!"

Occasionally the more temperamental actors resented the exuberance with which Josh entered into their roles. In such cases a more gentle approach might have won them over. But Josh was simply being himself and most actors loved him for it.

Theatrical directors, with rare exceptions like Josh, succeed by means of adroit diplomacy. Once Dudley Nichols, the movie director, wasn't satisfied with the way Rosalind Russell, the star, played a scene. He said, "Wonderful! Wonderful! But I could see, Miss Russell, when you hesitated that brief instant, that you were thinking about the possibility of playing the scene just a trifle lower key. Shall we try it once the way you were thinking?"

PERSUASIVE QUESTIONS

"Have you considered this?" is better than "No, you're doing it wrong," unless you are talking to someone who has deep faith in you. "Do you think this would work?" may be better than "Here's what you should do." If you let the other fellow sell himself on your idea, he'll stay sold.

One of the great sales managers, Alfred E. Lyon of Philip Morris, Inc., never told a salesman how to improve, he only suggested. Instead of finding fault even by implication, he would ask, "Have you ever wanted to try it this way?" and would briefly describe the better way. His suggestions were usually tried out.

We can't all develop the delicacy of a Nichols or a Lyon, nor the exuberance of a Cromwell or a Logan. But we can develop the underlying emotion that helped them all to achieve greatness: sincere enthusiasm.

The way we show enthusiasm will depend somewhat on our own personalities—but show it we must if we want to work with people. The poker-faced type who talks in a cold monotone has two strikes on him. He takes it for granted that his words are enough, but words carry only a small part of the meaning. The tone of what is said and the expression of a speaker's face are more important than the words.

UNENTHUSIASTIC? THEN ENTHUSE!

Enthusiasm can be consciously *cultivated* until it becomes second nature. At first, when we don't feel enthused, we may have to force ourselves to smile and deliberately add warmth to our voice. But this pretense soon becomes genuine. When we put on an external show of enthusiasm, we can't help feeling better inside. Almost in spite of ourselves, we get the habit of enthusiasm.

"Assume a virtue if you have it not," Shakespeare advised, and went on to say that the virtue would thereupon begin to grow within you. The great Harvard psychologist William James explained the process more precisely:

> Action seems to follow feeling. But really action and feeling go together; and by regulating the action, which is under the more direct control of the will, we can indirectly regulate the feeling, which is not.
> Thus the sovereign voluntary path to cheerfulness, if our cheerfulness be lost, is to sit up cheerfully and to act and speak as if cheerfulness were already there.

Try it for yourself. It works.

As we said in the beginning, salesmen seldom realize their full potentialities. They need someone to cheer them on, so they won't get frightened or discouraged into a half-hearted effort. George Hopkins, founder of the Society of American Sales Executives, used to point out that a good salesman is "emotional" and "will, when at his best, assume that the customer wants to buy. When he feels this way, he sells. When he makes preparation for failure, he fails."

Feelings are contagious. A salesman's confidence in the outcome helps to produce a Yes response from his prospect.

And a sales manager's confidence in his men helps to produce a "can do" spirit in them.

So pump up that good feeling, and make it felt!

11-- PERSUASION FROM THE PLATFORM

Running a Sales Meeting

Young Abe Lincoln may have been talking for his life one night in southern Illinois. He stood before a huge crowd that had seriously threatened to "nail his hide to a barn door" if he spoke against slavery.

This was the area where a mob of pro-slavery fanatics had put Elijah Lovejoy's abolitionist newspaper out of business by murdering him; where Lincoln himself had been challenged to a duel for a letter he had, written to a newspaper. So the rising young maverick politician must have been scared as he rose to speak.

Nevertheless, he handled the situation adroitly. And there are lessons for every public speaker in what he did.

Notice his opening sentence as he began slowly: "Fellow citizens of southern Illinois, fellow citizens of the state of Kentucky, fellow citizens of Missouri."

He was identifying himself with his audience—establishing the fact that he had much in common with them. This is a primary aim of any good speech, especially when talking to people likely to be skeptical and unfriendly. One of the fundamentals of all persuasion is to create a friendly atmosphere.

187

Then, in his next few sentences, Lincoln went on to recognize the unfavorable situation and adjust harmoniously to it:

"I'm told there are some of you here present who would like to make trouble for me. I don't understand why they should. I'm a plain, common man, like the rest of you. And why should I not have as good a right to speak my sentiments as the rest of you?"

Who could quarrel with this? Nobody could say that the Congressman was putting on airs, or trying to show off, or making any threats or demands. Yet he wasn't pleading or whining either. (Notice, too how Lincoln made his listeners feel that they weren't the ones who opposed him. Three times he spoke of "you" but when he mentioned his opposition he used a different pronoun: "they.")

Warming to the theme of his opening sentence, he dwelt on his similarity to his listeners:

"Why, good friends, I am one of you! I'm not an interloper here. I was born in Kentucky, and raised in Illinois, just like the most of you, and worked my way along by hard scratching. I know the people of Kentucky, and I know the people of southern Illinois, and I think I know the Missourians. I'm one of them, and therefore ought to know them."

Then Lincoln moved smoothly into his renewed appeal for a sympathetic hearing:

"—and they ought to know me better, and if they did know me better, they would know that I'm not disposed to make them trouble. Then why should they, or any of them, want to make trouble for me? Don't do any such foolish thing, fellow citizens. Let us be friends, and treat each other like friends. I am one of the humblest and most peaceful men in the world— would wrong no man, would interfere with no man's rights. And all I ask is that, having something to say, you give me a decent hearing."

He then paused to toss in additional compliments—which persuasive speakers usually do several times in the early minutes of a speech—and went on to begin his sales talk for the abolition of slavery:

"And, being Illinoisians, Kentuckians, and Missourians— brave and gallant people—I feel sure you will do that. And now let us reason together, like the honest fellows we are."

After that the crowd was with Lincoln all the way. He had given them mental pictures of themselves as gallant, honest, his friends, and his long-time neighbors. It was easy for them to sit and "reason together" with this homely stranger whom they had been ready to lynch a few minutes earlier.

Lincoln was using a principle that he followed throughout his public life. "If you would win a man to your cause you must first convince him that you are his sincere friend," he said once. At another time he put it slightly differently: "The best way to destroy an enemy is to make him a friend."

In every chapter of this book we've seen how necessary it is to get in step with the people we want to persuade; as long as they feel unfriendly they won't really listen. In speaking to a group, creating a friendly atmosphere is even more vital—and more difficult—than in other human situations. Usually we need to go further to establish ourselves as a regular guy, someone very much like our listeners.

Shakespeare knew this. In his play *Julius Caesar,* he shows Mark Antony, a famous orator, facing a hostile mob that has just seen Caesar assassinated, to its great satisfaction. See how similar Mark Antony's approach is to Abe Lincoln's. He begins by identifying himself with his audience: "Friends, Romans, countrymen!" Then he recognizes the ugly situation, and implies that he's on the crowd's side: "I come to bury Caesar, not to praise him."

Having gotten the crowd with him, Mark Antony slowly begins to swing it around to an opposite way of thinking about its dead ruler: "The evil that men do lives after them. The good is oft interred with their bones. So let it be with Caesar. The noble Brutus hath told you Caesar was ambitious. If it were so, it was a grievous fault—and grievously hath Caesar answered it. . . . Brutus is an honorable man. So are they all—all honorable men."

Before Mark Antony finishes, he has the crowd howling "O noble Caesar! O woeful day! We'll burn the house of Brutus!" His speech, as written by Shakespeare, is a masterpiece in the art of crowd conversion. You'd enjoy going back and reading it in full.

GETTING A CROWD TO ACCEPT YOU

Big-city attorneys, when they try a case before a small-town jury, wear old and shabby suits. Politicians on a campaign tour take pains to show as much familiarity as they can with the home folks' points of pride: They start with compliments on the climate and the scenery, on local boys who made good, on the victories of the local athletic team, on the great traditions and customs of the area.

Even if they don't speak the same language as their audience, they seek ways of establishing kinship. For example, when General Leonard Wood was sent to Cuba as governor of the conquered territory after the Spanish-American War, he began his job of winning over the resentful Cubans by showing his respect for the Catholic Church, which they revered. He was a Protestant but he walked the streets of Santiago solemnly swinging a Catholic censer. A Catholic canopy shaded his head, a mitered bishop walked beside him. The crowds cheered.

Similarly, when William Howard Taft went to the Philippines after the same war, to sell new plans of government to the hostile Filipinos, he studied their fast-stepping dance called the rigadon. Night after night as he toured the provinces he guided his famous bulk nimbly through the rigadon's complexities with light-footed Filipino beauties. "This man was irresistible," wrote

Abe Lincoln

reporter Oscar Davis. "He found the Filipinos sullen, suspicious. . . . He made them all friends."

It may be hackneyed but it's never stale to start a speech with remarks like "I was born and grew up here, and I'm one of you" or, "I too am an engineer" or golfer or poker-player or whatever else the speaker may have in common with most of his audience. And it's always sound salesmanship to identify with the audience's beliefs: "Like you, I want our company to grow and prosper," or "I too believe in better schools," or "All of us here hate drugs."

WHY MAKE SPEECHES?

As a sales manager, you probably won't ever face such unfriendly mobs as did Lincoln or Mark Antony or Taft. Yet no sales manager can afford to assume that a meeting of his salesmen will radiate good will toward him.

One of the key reasons for calling a sales meeting is to bolster sagging morale. Salesmen are emotional people or they wouldn't be salesmen. And emotional people have ups and downs. A salesman alone in the field too long is likely to get depressed by the grumbling of customers. He gets to thinking that the company's prices really are too high or the quality isn't good enough or deliveries are scandalously slow. The competition just seems to be getting altogether too tough. And he wonders why his expense allowances aren't more generous. Why doesn't the company do more and better advertising? Why is he required to do so much paperwork? Why shouldn't he have a better territory? Salesmen prey to such negative thoughts can be a tough audience for you.

Then, too, there are the older, fatter, contented salesmen who merely go on taking orders from their old established customers. They need to be stimulated to dig up new accounts, against the day when old customers may fade away. Therefore another function of a sales meeting is to stir up the satisfied salesmen to greater efforts. Which is not an easy assignment for you, on the platform facing them.

A generation or two ago, the old idea of master and servant was supposed to describe the relationship between sales manager and salesman. The manager gave commands; the salesman was expected to obey without question. It took business a long time to realize that high morale was essential to good selling, and that a boss couldn't build morale by merely issuing orders.

Consequently, business now finds sales meetings so essential that it spends upwards of $150 million yearly on them. Much of this money may be wasted on poorly-run meetings. That's why salesmen often mutter, "The trouble with selling is you have to go to so damned many sales meetings." Some sales meetings or conventions are held just to satisfy the bosses' yen for "speechifying," or to give the boys a good time, or simply because "It's time we had another one."

Yet some sales meetings must pay off or increasingly cost-conscious companies wouldn't continue to foot the bill. A good meeting has a well-defined purpose. It may be to educate, inspire, enthuse, explain the product, explain the offer, explain the salesmen's job, or to announce important news—any or all of these.

"Good salesmen need more than just a big commission," says Bill Morton, vice-president of a New York firm that specializes in dreaming up high-powered programs for sales meetings. "They need motivation. A good meeting can supply them with psychic income that makes them feel they're an important part of the team."

Some companies' sales meetings are extravaganzas with bands, movies, huge displays, fancy costumes, and special effects of all kinds. Far be it from me to belittle razzle-dazzle, since I've used so much of it in my own career. But I do think that somewhere in the course of every program the sales manager should stand up and talk to his men—enthusiastically, informatively, and persuasively. If he doesn't do this he is likely to seem insignificant to the men he is trying to manage. Each sales meeting is, in addition to other things, a chance for the sales manager to sell himself.

FEAR IS A FRIEND

Facing this challenge, you probably feel scared. That's good. It means you're keyed up, which you need to be.

A wholesome fear of failure is a good lift toward success. As Captain Ahab decreed in *Moby Dick*, "I will have no man on my boat who does not fear a whale." Broadway actors with a lifetime of experience still quake and perspire before each performance of a long-running play. Star athletes worry when they no longer feel butterflies in their stomachs before a game.

These expert performers anticipate and welcome the jitters. So do expert speakers. They know that nothing is worse than feeling too sure of themselves before an important effort, because that's when they're most likely to go flat. The psychological principle is summed up by Ralph W. Gerard, professor of neurophysiology at the University of Michigan:

"A little anxiety is good for you. It brings into use brain cells otherwise inactive. It heightens attention, improves performance, releases certain hormones, and facilitates learning by a greater spread of nerve messages in the brain."

Hasn't your own experience confirmed this? You can probably remember times when you were in a tough spot and responded by rising above yourself.

So when you're getting ready to talk to a tough audience, accept your fear as nature's way of protecting you and helping you. Don't condemn yourself for your nervousness. Let those butterflies work for you. Let them drive you to prepare yourself thoroughly. Knowledge and preparation are the complete remedy for your jitters. You'll feel in command of yourself as soon as you start to talk.

Ralph C. Smedley, founder of Toastmasters International (the club in which men conquer fear of public speaking by doing it every week) says: "If the novice knows that he knows his subject, he has taken the first step in the conquest of fear. Knowledge inspires self-confidence, and knowledge plus confidence will overcome fear. The unprepared speaker has a right to be scared. His own neglect imposes the fear based on ignorance."

When you know your subject, you'll surprise yourself by your ability to speak extemporaneously about it. (I need hardly point out that a written speech at a sales meeting is worse than no speech at all; it stamps you as a man who lacks confidence. Reading a speech to salesmen would be as bad as reading a sales talk to a prospect.) A famous example is Daniel Webster's 1830 speech in the Senate, replying to Senator Bob Hayne of South Carolina who powerfully advocated state sovereignty and nullification of the Constitution.

Webster had only overnight to prepare his long reply, and gave it from brief notes. Yet it has been remembered ever since as one of the most eloquent speeches ever heard ("Liberty *and* Union, now and forever, one and inseparable!") and was a key factor in putting off war between the North and South for a whole generation.

"How could you prepare such a masterpiece overnight?" another Senator asked him afterward.

Webster answered, "I didn't. My whole life has been a preparation for that effort."

Webster merely assembled his thoughts overnight. But he drew on a lifelong knowledge of history and the Constitution, and on a lifetime of practice in impromptu speaking. Public speaking is like playing second base, or riding a bicycle, or any other feat of skill. With practice and experience, it becomes easier for you to react automatically to each new public-speaking situation as it arises.

Since being a good speaker is an important part of being a good sales manager, you'll want to practice often. Seize all the

speaking opportunities that came along, inside and outside of
business. You may never make a great speech, but you'll make
some good ones that will enlighten and enthuse your salesmen.

ANOTHER FRIEND: FUN

What's more, you'll have fun. It's fun to talk to a group and
get them smiling, get them wagging their heads, get them moving to the measure of your thoughts.

Don't overlook this point. Even though it has serious purposes, a sales meeting should be fun for the salesmen. If you're
having fun yourself, your men will feel it.

Remember the advice of the great psychologist, William
James, at the end of Chapter 10: The path to cheerfulness is to
act cheerfully. So if at first you're not having fun running the
meeting, pretend you are anyway. Move around animatedly.
Smile if it kills you. You're glad to be there. It's a chance to help
this group. Think how long it would take to train everyone here
if you had to work with them individually. So you make yourself look happy and soon you feel happy, and so does the audience.

Remember that your audience, while it may be cold when you
start to speak, would subconsciously prefer to warm up. No
normal person chooses to be bored and unhappy, if he has a
choice.

A successful sales manager, Archie McLachlan, often pointed
out that men and women are "only kids grown up." It's a helpful
way of thinking about them. A persuasive leader tends to look
on his followers as lovable, emotional children. He is interested
in what he can cause them to feel, not in his own feelings at the
moment.

Let's look further into this point. A successful speech is a
group sale. And selling is teaching, communicating information
so well that the listener understands it and acts upon it. When

you think of yourself as a teacher, you'll plan better meetings.

Look into the history of teaching and you'll find that the first group of great teachers were the schoolmasters of the Renaissance. They were enthusiastic believers in the civilizing powers of education, and their schools sprang up and thrived all over western Europe from about 1450 onward. If you judge them by the pupils they produced, they were sensationally successful. How did they succeed? How did they get the young to learn such hard subjects as Latin, Greek, and math?

We're told that they succeeded mainly because they themselves loved the subjects so much and talked so excitingly about them. Because the teachers were having fun, their pupils had fun too. Students called the masters "magicians" and begged them to go on and on, while listeners "gathered up every word like pearls."

In addition, the best Renaissance teachers spurred on their pupils by various appeals to what educators call the play-principle. They made learning entertaining by making it purposeful play. (Vittorino da Feltre called his spectacularly successful school Jollity House—*La Casa Giocosa*.) They encouraged their boys to compete with each other, rewarding them with praise and prizes. They invented games to put more fun into hard subjects. Montaigne's father, for instance, started him on Greek as a child by writing the letters on cards, and made up a game to play with them; others taught mathematics in the same way.

The same basic principle helps many successful sales managers. They put the play-principle into their meetings. They may stage a contest to see which salesman can give the best demonstration of the product, or who can make the best sales talk to a pretended tough customer. They pose knotty sales problems and give prizes for the best answers.

They even make a game out of the grim formality of checking up on attendance. Perhaps they'll have each man make a little speech introducing himself (since it helps to put any group at ease if everyone knows everyone else). Perhaps they also have each man write his name on a dollar bill and drop it into a big bowl. Everyone is told there will be a drawing at the end of the meeting, and the man whose bill is drawn wins the pot. The catch is that the man whose bill is drawn must summarize the meeting to the satisfaction of all present. "It sure keeps everyone taking notes," says Oscar Wilkerson, president of a New Jersey firm that specializes in planning and producing sales meetings.

After the Renaissance schoolmen, another group of great teachers developed other fine teaching methods. These were the Jesuit fathers of the early eighteenth century. They were meticulous planners. They made sure the pupils realized what they were doing and why. But they were careful not to let the lessons get cut and dried.

Again and again the Jesuits impressed on their teachers the fact that pupils differ, classes differ, ages differ; the teacher's duty is to adapt himself to the unique group of boys he sees in front of him. In a vivid image, Father Jouvancy said that a schoolboy's mind is like a narrownecked bottle. It can take in a huge amount of learning, but only in little drops; so go slowly. Father Possevino added another image (the Jesuits were great on teaching with mental pictures): Boys are like salt, sugar, flour, and chalk—much alike at first glance, but deeply different in essence, and all useful. So the teacher must discover their differences, and adapt his teaching to them as far as he can.

A SPEAKER-SALESMAN IN ACTION

I once heard a wise old teacher say, "I consider my day's teaching is wasted if we don't all have at least one hearty laugh." He knew that when people laugh together, they stop being teacher and students, boss and employees, speaker and audience. They fuse together as a single group of human beings enjoying their own existence.

That's why good sales managers put laughs into every sales meeting. Let's listen to one of the best, Bob Longtoft, as he starts talking to his men:

"It's good to have you guys come in from all over the territory for these sales meetings. I *like* to see you! There isn't a man here who doesn't know that I genuinely like him personally."

See how careful he is to talk the language of his audience, and to create a friendly mood? His men already know him well. But he wants to keep reminding them that he's their friend. (As we've seen, this is important for any speaker who wants to move an audience to action.) Now Longtoft starts mixing in a few laughs on himself, which also are important:

"I call you 'my boys.' And some of you call me 'Pop' or 'the Old Man.' Sometimes when I trim the profit out of your expense accounts, you call me other things. But you know I'm always on the level with you. It makes me proud when you smile and say, 'Same old Bob!' I know that sometimes to shorten this, you say 'S.O.B.' "

In this genial way, not putting on an act; just being himself, Longtoft is nevertheless subtly softening up his audience for some stiff demands. He plans to insist that his men work harder. His S.O.B. joke is the first hint that this is coming. Now he follows with more hints, also sugar-coated as jokes:

But we understand one another, and you're still my boys —even though I occasionally have to let some of you know you are of the illegitimate variety. Now, the one thing that a father wants is to be proud of his boys.

For example, the state prison warden told one of my neighbors that his son was getting out of the pen six months early on account of his good behavior. My neighbor said, "I *knew* my boy would make good!"

Another proud father in the Carolina mountains told the census taker that his boy was down at the state university. The census taker asked, "What is he studying?" The mountaineer threw out his chest and answered, "He ain't studyin' nothin'. They're studyin' *him!* He's got two heads."

The fathers in these two stories had one thing in common—they wanted so much to be proud of their children that they stretched a point to do it. Now, I want to be proud of my boys too. But when I look at your last quarter's sales record I have to do a hell of a lot of stretching.

If this were a group of strangers, Longtoft would need to throw in some compliments to them. However, these men already know from experience that he esteems them. So he skips the bouquets and gets down to business. But notice how careful he is to maintain a semi-kidding atmosphere:

"Frankly, the reason I'm so glad to see you this morning is that I thought some of you had died. We had company life insurance checks ready to mail to your wives. I see Howard Stickly here with his arm in a sling. That explains why he hasn't been able to write any orders. But we're going to find out in the next three days why the rest of you haven't been writing any.

"If there's any man here who thinks he knows all about selling, let him stand and say so. The rest of you are going to learn how. The vacation is over, boys. School is starting *now!*"

Longtoft doesn't call his men lazy or stupid. He knows better than to antagonize them by such a verbal flogging. Instead he implies that his men will do better when they learn how. So he keeps them on his side. They are in a receptive mood, ready to learn.

Another sales manager might not dare to use such rough humor as Longtoft did. His men might bristle if he said that he'd thought some of them were dead, or that some called him an

S.O.B. behind his back. Longtoft knew his audience, and they knew him. The jokes fitted the free-and-easy character they knew. So no one took offense.

IT HELPS TO KID YOURSELF

As a general rule, though, it's safer to keep the humor aimed at yourself. Cervantes warned, "Jests that slap the face are not good jests." Therefore most sales managers and others who speak often in public are prepared with jokes that let the audience feel a bit superior to them.

Albert Lasker, who built a great advertising agency, brought in most of its big accounts himself. Whenever he began his talk to skeptical executives of a prospective client company, he would get them chuckling by this kind of beginning: "Gentlemen, I am an advertising man—so you had better watch me closely."

Other seasoned speakers often get a laugh by pretending to blunder at the start of a speech. I remember one executive who took out a bulky manuscript and began reading aloud, "Today you come to another millstone in the life of your company . . . millstone?" He threw away the manuscript, while the audience roared, and launched into the impromptu talk he'd planned to give all along.

Another veteran sales speaker, Gene Flack, used a favorite gag at the beginning of talks to business groups. He would take out some notes, glance at them, and begin, "Mr. Chairman, honored guests, and fellow members of the Teamsters Union— uh, pardon me, ladies and gentlemen, that's my speech for *tomorrow* night." It always got a laugh, and Gene built on it with a series of funny remarks about how confused a speaker could get. From this he could lead smoothly into whatever his subject happened to be that evening.

Most successful politicians are especially quick with quips that turn a laugh on themselves. We all remember President Kennedy's response to a press-conference question about whether he had seen something in the newspapers, "Yes, I've been reading more and enjoying it less." He was a witty man, but a joke as good as this may well have been one he thought up in advance and saved for the right moment.

The 300-pound H. Roe Bartle, a widely-known public speaker, begins every speech with jokes about his own tonnage. He can get any audience laughing. This ability was a real factor in making him a two-term mayor of Kansas City, a college president, and a director of seventeen corporations.

Of course joking can be dangerous. A speaker may joke too much. Adlai Stevenson was naturally so witty that he was criticized for putting too much humor into his political speeches. One reporter on his campaign train wrote, "After listening to this man's speeches I can't figure whether his objective is the Presidency or a six-week contract at the Roxy Theater."

However, some of our most dignified public figures, who were in danger of seeming too serious, were wise enough to keep a few jokes about themselves on tap. The stiff-faced General John J. Pershing, who headed the American Expeditionary Forces in World War I, liked to start speeches with a remark about the days when he commanded troops in Mexico chasing Villa. He recalled that one of his scouts told him, "As I figure it, General, we've got Villa entirely surrounded—on one side."

And Woodrow Wilson, at an early turning point in his career, started a speech with a funny story that warmed up an unfriendly yet important audience. Soon after being elected governor of New Jersey, he was introduced at a New York banquet as "future President of the United States." The audience bridled visibly.

Wilson realized this. He began, "I find myself in one respect (I hope in only one respect) resembling certain persons I heard of in a story that was repeated to me the other day." The story went that a member of a fishing party imbibed too freely, and when he went to the railroad station to start home with the rest of the party, he jumped aboard the wrong train. His companions telegraphed the train's conductor: SEND SHORT MAN NAMED JOHNSON BACK FOR THE NORTHBOUND TRAIN. HE IS INTOXICATED. Presently the conductor wired them: FURTHER PARTICULARS NEEDED. THIRTEEN MEN ON THIS TRAIN DON'T KNOW EITHER THEIR NAME OR THEIR DESTINATION.

Then came Wilson's punchline: "Now, I am sure that I know my name. But I'm not so sure as your presiding officer that I know my destination."

Similarly, President Franklin D. Roosevelt took time on a nationwide broadcast to start with a story about an elderly listener to his previous speeches, whose doctor warned the old man that he must stop drinking or lose his hearing. According to the President, the old man said, "Well, I've thought it all over. I've decided that I like what I've been drinkin' so much better than I like what I've been hearin' that I reckon I'll just keep on gittin' deaf."

Chuck Sexauer, a Los Angeles politician I used to know, made a joke of his own name as he responded to introductions. He said that a credit bureau, trying to check up on him, phoned a business office and asked, "Do you have a Sexauer down there?" The telephone girl replied, "No indeed. We don't even get a coffee break here."

Remembering Mark Twain's remark that it took him about three weeks to prepare a good impromptu speech, you'll be wise to stock your mind in advance with a few little jokes about yourself, as well as other pleasant remarks you may need for your opening. Even though you won't be reading a speech nor trying to deliver a memorized one, you ought to have your first few sentences clearly in mind when you rise to speak.

FINISH STRONG

It's also wise to have your closing sentence ready before you begin. This is the sentence you want to leave in your listeners' minds.

William Gladstone, the great Parliamentary orator after whom the young Churchill patterned himself, said that whenever he rose to speak, he had two sentences memorized: the first and the last. Many famous speakers evidently follow the same rule. Their closing sentence is usually a sledgehammer climax that has been carefully planned in advance.

We've already quoted the final words of Webster's reply to Hayne. In completing another famous speech that electrified a national convention and won him the nomination for President, William Jennings Bryan roared, "We will answer their demand for a gold standard by saying to them: You shall not press down upon the brow of labor this crown of thorns; you shall not crucify mankind upon a cross of gold." His speech was remembered for decades as the Cross of Gold speech, although he didn't introduce the phrase until the last three words of his last sentence.

Winston Churchill was the great virtuoso of the powerful closing. He almost invariably had one. The day after the remnants of the British Army fled Europe and left Hitler in full control of the continent, Churchill made his immortal speech that ended, "We shall not flag nor fail. We shall go on to the end . . . we shall fight on the beaches, we shall fight on the landing grounds, we shall fight in the fields and in the streets, we shall fight in the hills, we *shall never surrender*."

And who could forget the Prime Minister's ringing summons to his people to begin the Battle of Britain? It concluded, "Let us therefore brace ourselves to our duties, and so bear ourselves that, if the British Empire and its Commonwealth last for a thousand years, men will say, 'This was their finest hour.' "

Put your central thought and your deep feeling into your last sentence. Sweep your audience with you to a strong climax. Give it all you have.

DEAL THE AUDIENCE A HAND

Having planned your opening and closing, and having thought out the points you want to make in the body of your speech (and perhaps summarized them on a card or two of notes), there is still much more that you can do in advance to make your meeting go over big.

For example, you can figure out ways to get your audience to take part.

We all enjoy taking part. We like to yell and clap at ball games, to cheer, to get into the act. So, as Ed Hegarty, the notably successful Westinghouse sales manager, used to phrase it, "To conduct a successful sales meeting, deal the audience a hand."

One way to do this is with a "Wisdometer" such as the Shelby Book Company uses at sales meetings. It's a board with fifty questions about Shelby products and policies. The questions are masked with tape. In turn, salesmen pull the questions. A few may turn out not to be a question but a lucky break: "For pulling off this question collect one dollar from the sales manager, and try another question." Others are tough problems such as "What is the cost of an extra color on Shelby form number 60?" A salesman may make a wild guess, "Five dollars per thousand," at which the chairman rings a gong and announces, "Sorry, you're wrong. You can't use a color on schedule 60." The meeting quizzes itself through dozens of questions with everyone enjoying themselves—and learning at the same time.

There are many simple little tricks to get an audience participating. You can ask early in your talk, "How many of you have trouble with So-and-so? Raise your hands." Or you can call on someone and ask, "Jim, what do you do about So-and-so? . . . Why do you do it that way?"

Or you may simply say, "I know Tom White agrees with this, don't you, Tom?" Or you can highlight an unfamiliar fact by saying, "We have a brand new element in our product now: a temperature differential," and then turning to someone and asking, "Bill, have you any idea what our engineers mean by a temperature differential?"

After giving the main points of your presentation, before winding up with your smash finish, you can change pace and pull the audience in by saying something like this: "Gentlemen, I think we've all gotten a lot from our discussion this morning, which makes me want to pin down some of our ideas all the more tightly. I wonder if you'll help me write on the blackboard the two, three, or four major points we've covered. Let's see, our first point was . . . ." If nobody answers immediately, look inquiringly at some specific person in the front rows who has shown special interest, and he'll probably supply the missing words.

THE EYE REMEMBERS WHAT THE EAR FORGETS

Notice that this doubles the impression on your audience. Not only do you say it for their ears to hear, but you write it for their eyes to see. Teachers use blackboards a great deal. Sales managers should do the same. People would rather look than listen. And they remember more of what they see than what they hear.

Even a minister in the pulpit can use visual props to drive home his message. I remember one who started a sermon by showing his congregation a locked cashbox. "The most important thing in life can't be kept safe in this box no matter how strong it is," he said.

The audience looked mystified, as he intended. He reached

for a preserve jar. "Can this jar or any other—even with the tightest lid—contain this precious something?"

He shook his head. Then he reached beneath his robe and turned out his empty jacket pocket, moving to the side of the pulpit so that everyone saw it. He said, "No pocket, no hand, no vault can hold it. This mysterious something that *can* be held— what is it?"

He paused while the audience waited, every eye on him. "It is the peace of mind that the Lord's presence assures!"

He was off to a good start. In his conclusion, he returned to his visual props—the cashbox, the jar and the turned-out pocket —as symbols of tangible possessions "far less important than the peace of mind which you can feel without having to touch!"

I once saw a sales meeting at which a girl dressed in old-fashioned long skirts came out from the wings and whispered to the speaker. He ignored her and she went away. Soon she reappeared in slacks. Again he paid no attention. When she came onstage the third time she wore a bikini.

This time he stopped speaking, went to meet her, and listened attentively while she whispered to him. Then he turned to his audience and said, "You know what she told me? '*You've got to show it to sell it.*' And she sure is right, isn't she?" His point was far more vivid than he could have made it with words alone.

Charles L. Lapp, professor of marketing at Washington University, has a speech in which he sets up a stepladder on the rostrum. He calls the speech Six Steps to Sales Success. As he talks about each, he moves up another rung on the ladder. He also illustrates the speech with a series of hats that he puts on to exemplify various types of salemen.

Every time you engage the eye you quicken the attention of your audience. That's why experienced speakers are constantly gesturing, moving around, and doing something different. You can jerk an audience back to closer attention by suddenly shifting your position. You can pour a glass of water and drink it, maybe with a remark that "Every time I think about this subject

I get overheated" or, "I want to make this point as clear as this water."

You can tear up your notes. You can pull off your coat and necktie, if the occasion isn't too formal. You can whack the lectern. You can extend your arm and point to something.

Merely by stopping and staring at whisperers in the audience, you can obtain a deathly quiet. Your dramatic pause, waiting for silence, will put you in command and make your audience alert to hear what you'll say to break the silence.

PRECAUTIONS PAY OFF

Don't let your visual props compete with you for attention. Many speakers make the mistake of passing out samples, pictures, or printed matter before or during their speech. Then they feel irked because the audience looks at the material while the speech is going on.

Distribute literature at the end of a talk; keep it out of sight until then. If you want the men to see a sample, take it down among the men yourself and show it. Or hand it to a man in the center of the room, where most of the group can see it. Have this man stand up and demonstrate its use with you, so that everyone will be watching your sample at the same time. Then take the sample back and announce that it will be available for examination after the meeting. But never let anything be handed around among your audience while you're trying to talk; if you do, you'll lose the spotlight for several minutes. As for literature, don't expect people to pick it up on the way out. Station your helpers at the doors to hand it out and make sure that everyone takes it.

Get your back to the wall, with nobody behind you. If the company president or some other dignitary is on the stage behind you, try to get him to move out front while you're talking.

Otherwise, every time he moves a hand he'll distract attention from you. This is known among actors as "upstaging."

Anyone behind you is a continuous menace. If he looks bored, the audience will think your talk is boring. If he nods his head, that may be helpful, but the point is that he's stealing some of the audience's attention.

So take every precaution you can, in advance, to make sure that nothing will distract your listeners' attention while you speak. Try to have the audience with its back to the entrance of the room, so that latecomers won't be noticeable. If a meeting must be held in a showroom with a plate glass window, seat the audience with its back to the window; otherwise eyes will rove whenever anything moves across that window.

If you'll need assistants at a meeting, arrange for them in advance. Try to set up beforehand so that no helper will be working on props, or tinkering with a projector, during your talk. Keep your visuals and other props covered so they'll be a surprise when you show them. If you have to change the seating arrangement to set up a projector, to move a blackboard or an exhibit, call a recess while you do it.

And try to make sure your audience will have good air to breathe. I've heard many sales managers say something like, "I've been attending sales meetings for thirty years, but never once have I been in one where there was enough fresh air." If your meeting room isn't satisfactorily air-conditioned, you'd better call recesses, open windows, and let in fresh air. If this isn't possible, at least let the men move outside for a breather.

If you'll need a lectern, microphone, blackboard, or other facilities, don't take anyone's word that those will be available. Get to the room early and make sure. In fact, you'll probably want to check several days in advance on the seats, acoustics, and lighting, so that a change can be made if they're inadequate.

If you don't make sure of your ground ahead of time, you may find yourself—as some hapless speakers do—trying to run a convention session from the middle of a gymnasium, with the audience sitting in the bleachers at both sidelines. One try at this will suffice for a lifetime.

I once saw an assistant sales manager negotiating with a hotel mechanic for the oiling of squeaky restaurant carts he'd noticed during his reconnaissance of the banquet hall where his boss was scheduled to speak. If you have an assistant like that, you're blessed. Most sales managers have to handle all such precautions themselves.

Random noises can be ruinous. Clanging radiators, the clatter of dishes in an adjoining room, or carpenters' hammers nearby, will upset the audience even more than you. While listeners may sympathize with your predicament, they won't be able to pay close attention to you. So take a close look beforehand and make sure that no such nuisances will spoil your talk.

Making a speech is much like fighting a battle against a clever enemy: distraction. Only fools give odds to the enemy; professionals never do. You need undivided attention to help you put over your story. Fight to keep the full spotlight on yourself—it pays.